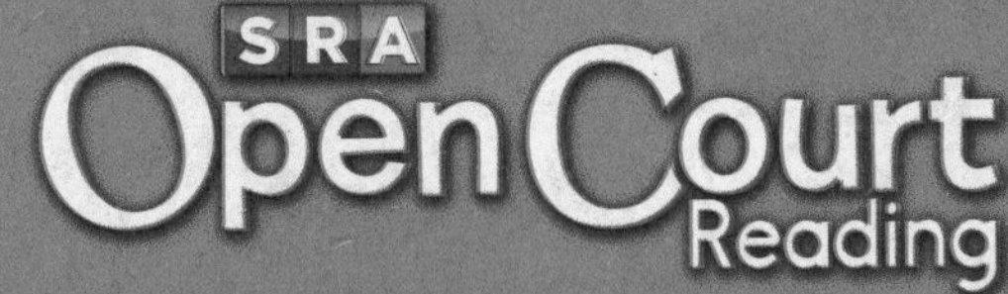

Core Decodable Takehomes

Core Decodables 63–114

Grade 1

Book 2

Bothell, WA • Chicago, IL • Columbus, OH • New York, NY

MHEonline.com

Send all inquiries to:
McGraw-Hill Education
8787 Orion Place
Columbus, OH 43240

ISBN: 978-0-07-672617-2
MHID: 0-07-672617-7

Printed in the United States of America.

8 9 10 11 12 13 QSX 24 23 22 21 20

Contents

About the Decodable Takehomes

The ***SRA Open Court Reading*** *Decodable Takehomes* allow your students to apply their knowledge of phonic elements to read simple, engaging texts. Each story supports instruction in a new phonic element and incorporates elements and words that have been learned earlier.

The students can fold and staple the pages of each *Decodable Takehome* to make books of their own to keep and read. We suggest that you keep extra sets of the stories in your classroom for the students to reread.

How to Make a Takehome

1. Tear out the pages you need.

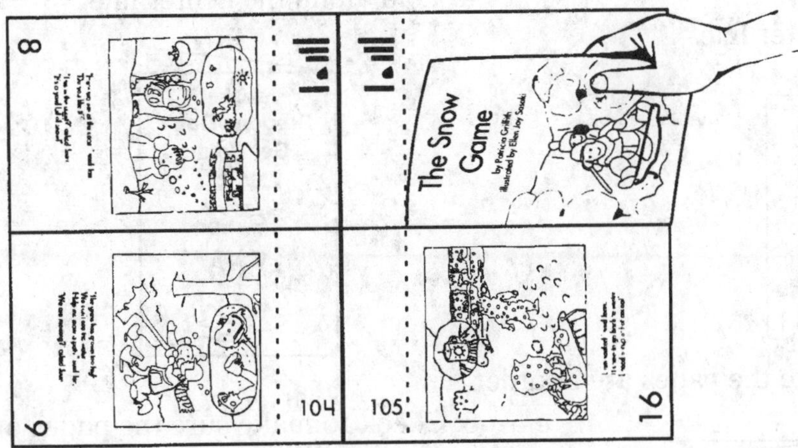

2. Place pages 4 and 5, and pages 2 and 7 faceup for 8-page books.

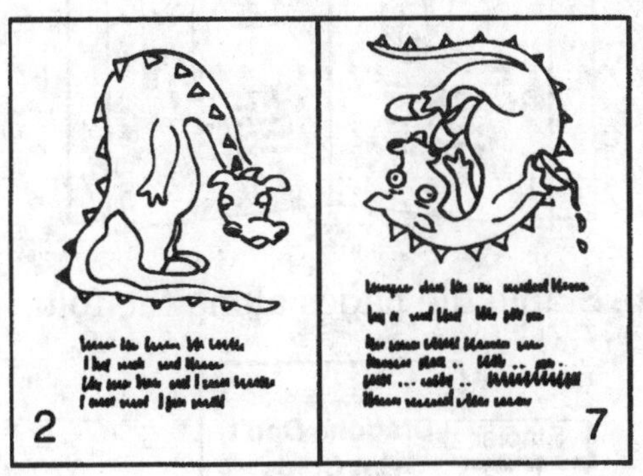

For 16-page book

3. Place the pages on top of each other in this order: pages 8 and 9, pages 6 and 11, pages 4 and 13, and pages 2 and 15.

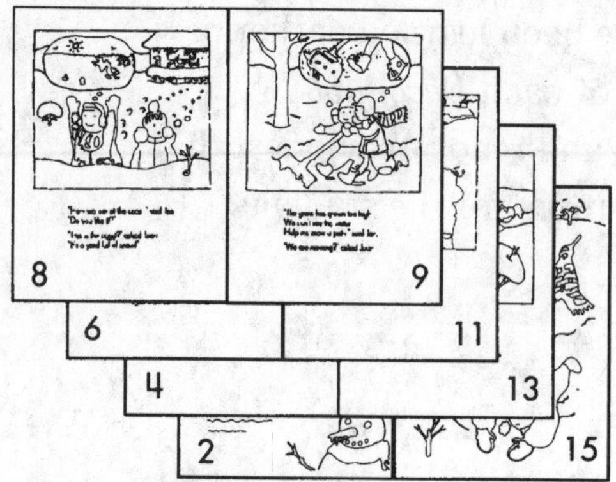

4. Fold along the center line.

5. Check to make sure the pages are in order.

6. Staple the pages along the fold.

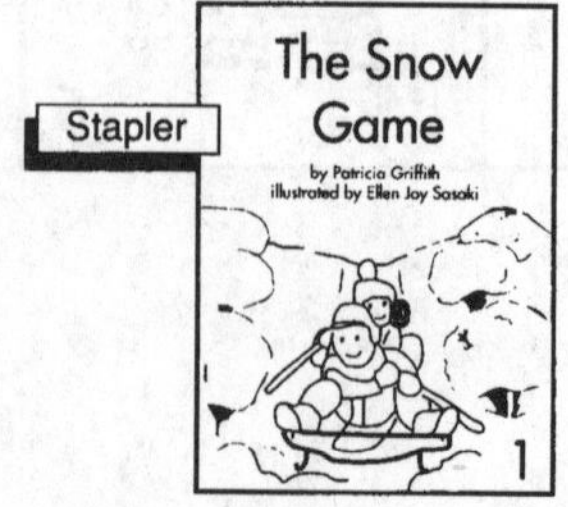

For 8-page book

3. Place pages 4 and 5 on top of pages 2 and 7.

4. Fold along the center line.

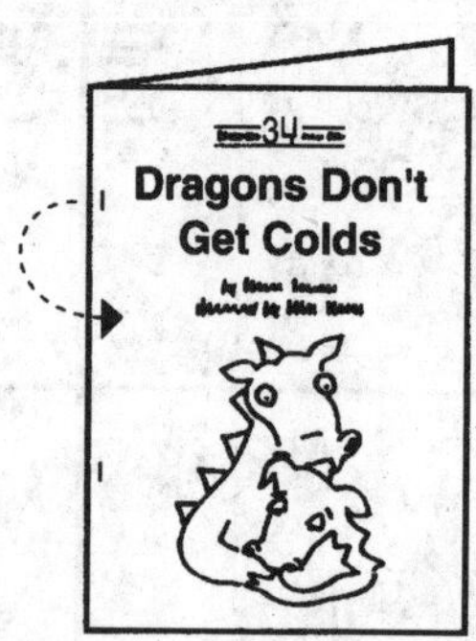

5. Check to make sure the pages are in order.

6. Staple the pages along the fold.

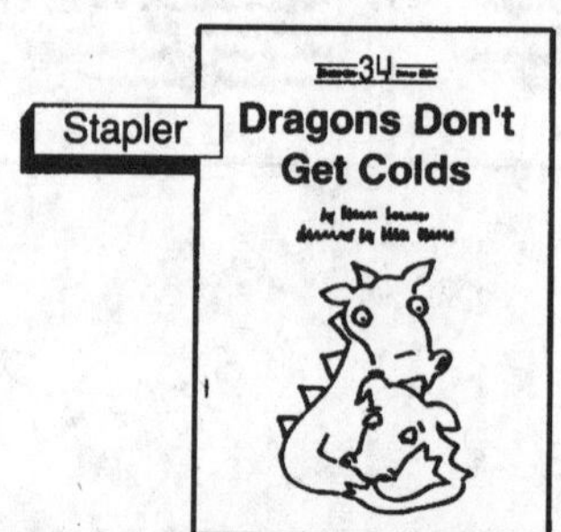

Just to let you know...

A message from ________________________________

Help your child discover the joy of independent reading with ***SRA Open Court Reading.*** From time to time your child will bring home his or her very own *Pre-Decodable* or *Decodable Takehomes* to share with you. With your help, these stories can give your child important reading practice and a joyful shared reading experience.

You may want to set aside a few minutes every evening to read these stories together. Here are some suggestions you may find helpful:

- Do not expect your child to read each story perfectly, but concentrate on sharing the book together.
- Participate by doing some of the reading.
- Talk about the stories you read, give lots of encouragement, and watch as your child becomes more fluent throughout the year!

Learning to read takes lots of practice. Sharing these stories is one way that your child can gain that valuable practice. Encourage your child to keep the *Pre-Decodable* or *Decodable Takehomes* in a special place. This collection will make a library of books that your child can read and reread. Take the time to listen to your child read from his or her library. Just a few moments of shared reading each day can give your child the confidence needed to excel in reading.

Children who read every day come to think of reading as a pleasant, natural part of life. One way to inspire your child to read is to show that reading is an important part of your life by letting him or her see you reading books, magazines, newspapers, or any other materials. Another good way to show that you value reading is to share a *Pre-Decodable* or *Decodable Takehome* with your child each day.

Successful reading experiences allow children to be proud of their newfound reading ability. Support your child with interest and enthusiasm about reading. You won't regret it!

High-Frequency Words

a	boy	from	I	now	sleep	was
about	brown	get	if	of	some	water
after	but	girl	in	old	take	way
all	by	go	into	on	that	we
am	call	going	is	one	the	well
an	came	good	it	or	their	went
and	can	got	its	out	them	were
any	come	green	jump	over	then	what
are	could	had	just	pretty	there	when
around	day	has	know	put	they	where
as	did	have	like	red	this	will
ask	do	he	little	ride	to	with
at	don't	help	long	right	too	would
away	down	her	look	said	two	yellow
be	every	here	make	saw	up	yes
before	five	him	me	see	very	you
big	for	his	my	she	walk	your
blue	four	how	no	six	want	

Sound/Spelling Correspondences in Core Decodables

1. Pre-decodable
2. Pre-decodable
3. Pre-decodable
4. Pre-decodable
5. Pre-decodable
6. /s/ spelled *s*, /m/ spelled *m*, /a/ spelled *a*
7. /t/ spelled *t, tt*
8. Review
9. /d/ spelled *d*
10. /n/ spelled *n*
11. /i/ spelled *i*
12. /h/ spelled *h_*
13. Review
14. /p/ spelled *p*
15. /l/ spelled *l, ll*
16. /o/ spelled *o*
17. /b/ spelled *b*
18. Review
19. /k/ spelled *c*
20. special spelling *al, all*
21. /k/ spelled *k,* ■*ck*
22. /r/ spelled *r*
23. Review
24. /f/ spelled *f, ff*
25. /s/ spelled *ss*
26. /g/ spelled *g*
27. /j/ spelled *j*
28. Review
29. /j/ spelled ■*dge*
30. /u/ spelled *u*
31. /z/ spelled *z, zz*
32. /z/ spelled *_s*
33. Review
34. /ks/ spelled ■*x*
35. /e/ spelled *e*
36. *-ed* ending: /ed/, /d/
37. *-ed* ending: /t/
38. Review
39. /e/ spelled *_ea_*
40. /sh/ spelled *sh*
41. /th/ spelled *th*
42. /ch/ spelled *ch,* ■*tch*
43. Review
44. /or/ spelled *or, ore*
45. /ar/ spelled *ar*
46. /w/ spelled *w_*
47. /w/ spelled *wh_*
48. Review
49. /er/ spelled *er, ir*
50. /er/ spelled *ur*
51. /er/ spelled *ear*
52. /ng/ spelled ■*ng*
53. Review
54. Schwa
55. *-le, -el, -il, -al*
56. /nk/ spelled ■*nk*
57. /kw/ spelled *qu_*
58. Review
59. /y/ spelled *y_*
60. /v/ spelled *v*
61. /ā/ spelled *a, a_e*
62. Review
63. /ī/ spelled *i, i_e*
64. /s/ spelled *ce, ci_*
65. /j/ spelled *ge, gi_*
66. Review
67. /ō/ spelled *o, o_e*
68. /ū/ spelled *u, u_e*
69. Review
70. /ē/ spelled *e, e_e*
71. /ē/ spelled *ee, ea*
72. Review /ē/
73. /ē/ spelled *_y, _ie_*
74. /ē/ spelled *_ey*
75. Review
76. /s/ spelled *cy*
77. /ā/ spelled *ai_, _ay*
78. Review
79. /ī/ spelled *_igh*
80. /ī/ spelled *_y, _ie*
81. Review /ī/
82. /ō/ spelled *oa_, _ow*
83. /ū/ spelled *_ew, _ue*
84. Review
85. /m/ spelled *_mb*
86. /n/ spelled *kn_, gn*
87. /r/ spelled *wr_*
88. /f/ spelled *ph*
89. Review
90. /o͞o/ spelled *oo*
91. /o͞o/ spelled *u, _ue*
92. Review
93. /o͞o/ spelled *_ew, u_e*
94. /oo/ spelled *oo*
95. Review
96. /ow/ spelled *ow*
97. /ow/ spelled *ou_*
98. /aw/ spelled *au_, aw*
99. Review
100. /aw/ spelled *augh, ough*
101. /oi/ spelled *oi, _oy*
102. Review
103. Prefixes *un-, dis-*
104. Prefixes *im-, in-, re-*
105. Review /ā/ and /a/
106. Review /ī/ and /i/
107. Review /ō/ and /o/
108. Review /ū/ and /u/
109. Review /ē/ and /e/
110. Review consonant digraphs
111. Review r-controlled vowels
112. Review /oo/ and /o͞o/
113. Review diphthongs
114. Review inflectional endings

We can ride bikes in the park.

Hikers can walk on a path.

A Mess

by Jan Stewart
illustrated by Anni Matsick

Core Decodable 63

Mc Graw Hill Education

Bothell, WA • Chicago, IL • Columbus, OH • New York, NY

MHEonline.com

McGraw Hill Education

Send all inquiries to:
McGraw-Hill Education
8787 Orion Place
Columbus, OH 43240

We picked up a lot.
We made a big junk pile.

This is a smashed kite.

This is a plastic pipe.

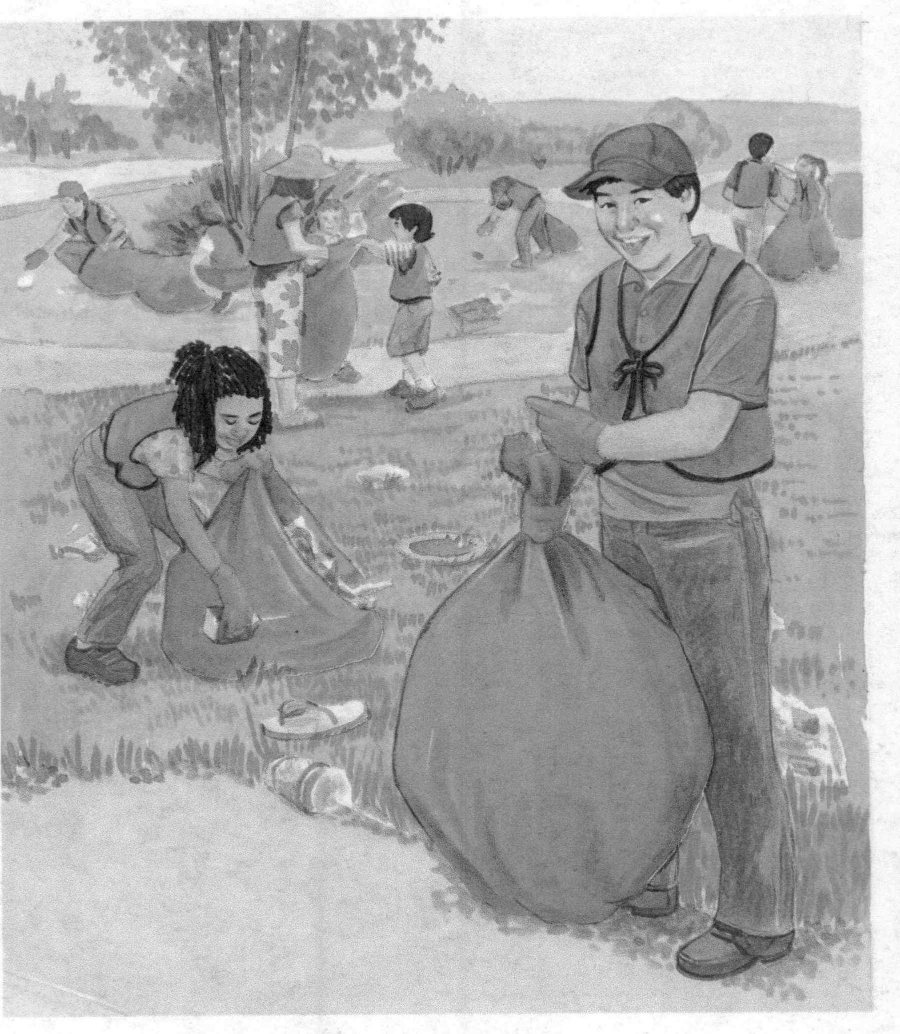

The park is a mess!

It is time to pick up.

What kind of trash did we find?
Well, we see a bike tire!

This wide bag is mine.
I filled it with paper.

Grace's pencil fell.
"I do not have the hands!"

Grace and Vince

by David Nguyen
illustrated by Jennifer Emery

Core Decodable 64

Bothell, WA • Chicago, IL • Columbus, OH • New York, NY

MHEonline.com

McGraw Hill Education

Send all inquiries to:
McGraw-Hill Education
8787 Orion Place
Columbus, OH 43240

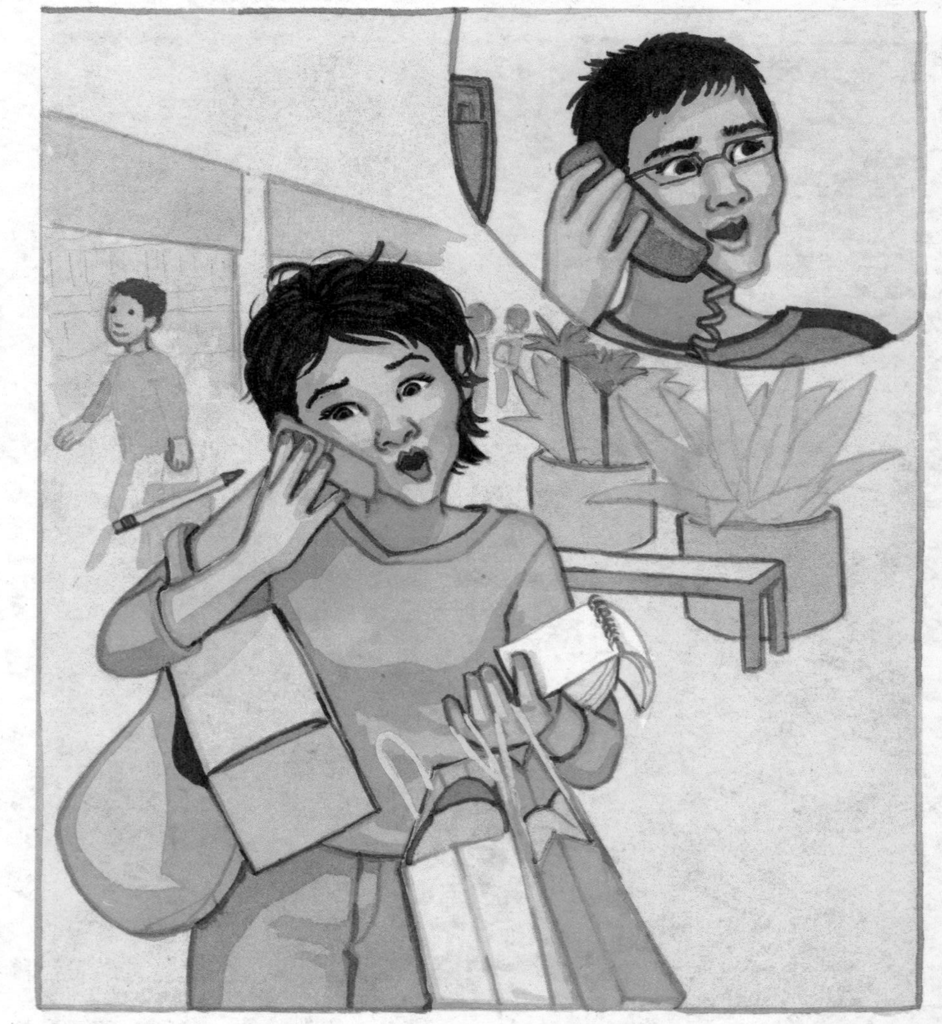

"I can't," Grace grinned.

"You do not have cash?" asked Vince.

"And citrus drinks and cider?" Vince added.

"Can you get them all?"

Grace shopped at Civic Center Mall.

Her cell rang. Vince called.

"Do you have a pencil?" Vince asked.
Grace smiled. "I do."

"Can you make a shopping list?
Ice, rice, spice?" asked Vince.

Ginger and Gem like Space Danger.
They will go back.

Ginger and Gem

by Emma Green
illustrated by Holly Jones

Core Decodable 65

Mc Graw Hill Education
Bothell, WA • Chicago, IL • Columbus, OH • New York, NY

MHEonline.com

McGraw Hill Education

Send all inquiries to:
McGraw-Hill Education
8787 Orion Place
Columbus, OH 43240

Go! Go! Go!

They like this part best!

The last stage is a large drop.
Ginger and Gem fall!

Ginger and Gem like this ride.
It is called Space Danger.

Ginger and Gem go up the giant ride.
This stage of the ride is gentle.

Then Ginger and Gem stop.
This is the second stage.

The path ends at the giant rock.
What a fun and wild ride!

Riding in Gem Park

by Antonio Colantoni
illustrated by Ellen Joy Sasaki

Core Decodable 66

Mc Graw Hill Education
Bothell, WA • Chicago, IL • Columbus, OH • New York, NY

MHEonline.com

Mc Graw Hill Education

Send all inquiries to:
McGraw-Hill Education
8787 Orion Place
Columbus, OH 43240

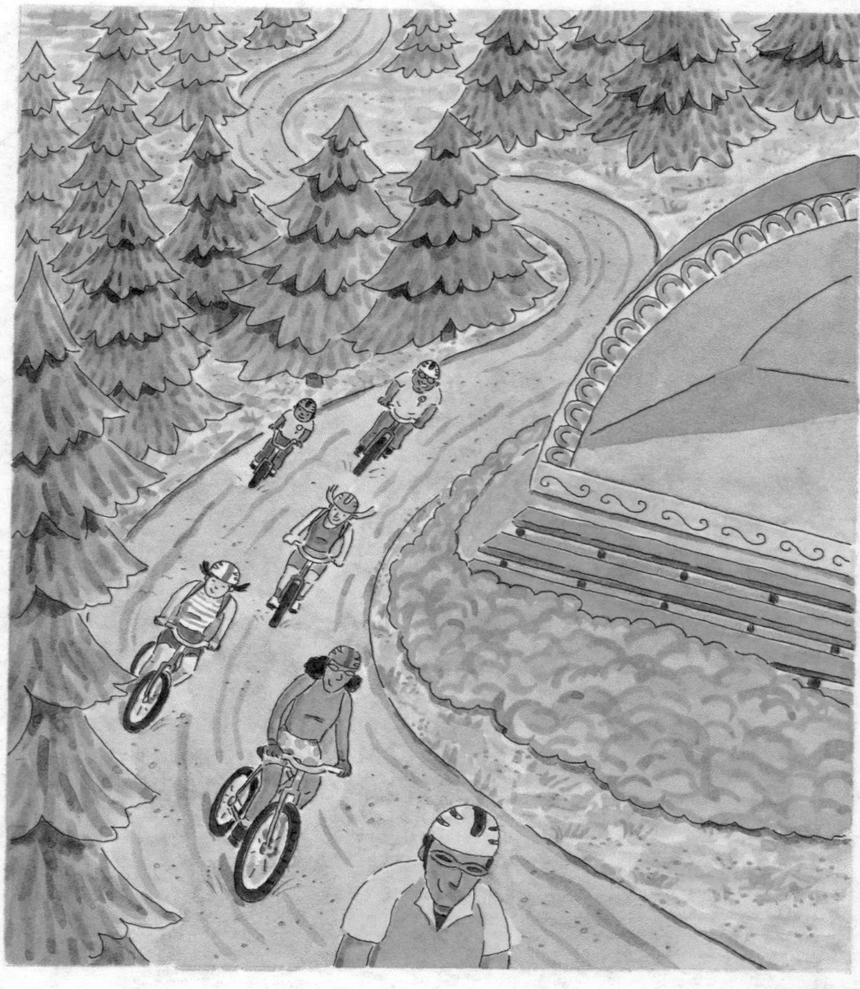

The path twists and turns.
It passes the concert shell.

Riders check bike brakes.
They will glide down fast.

Gem Park is a large park.
It has a nice bike path.

The path is flat at first.
And it is cement.

At the top, the path turns.
It starts down the hill.

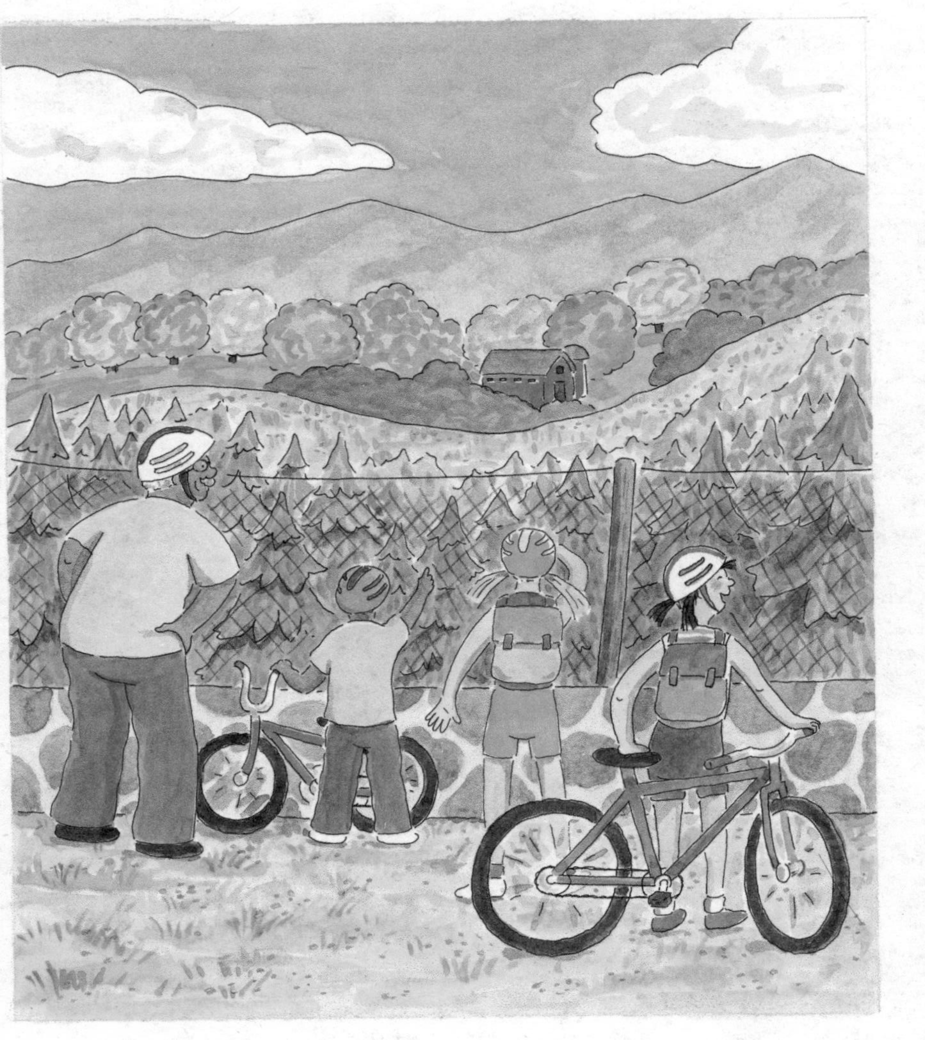

At the hilltop, it's quiet.
You see much in the distance.

The cement path lasts a mile.
It runs past Pine River.

After the bridge, the path changes.
It is not as flat.

The path is on a giant cliff.
A fence makes it safe.

If riders get tired, they rest.
They do not have to race.

The path is uphill.
And it is gravel and cinders.

The hill is gentle at first.
The ride is not bad.

Then the ride is hard.
Tires slip on the cinders.

Mom and Chad skated in the yard.
"I hope winter lasts!" said Chad.

Frozen

by Lucy Shepard
illustrated by Angela Adams

Core Decodable 67

Mc Graw Hill Education
Bothell, WA • Chicago, IL • Columbus, OH • New York, NY

MHEonline.com

Mc Graw Hill Education

Send all inquiries to:
McGraw-Hill Education
8787 Orion Place
Columbus, OH 43240

The entire yard had frozen.
Mom had made an ice rink!

Mom filled the open spot.

It froze hard. It froze so fast!

Chad felt sad and alone.

He wished winter was over.

Did Mom go out?
Did Mom have a hose?

Chad looked in his yard.
A big spot was open.

Muse did not like big branches on his back.
But Muse liked Hugo's music.

Muse the Mule

by Dottie Raymer
illustrated by Jan Pyk

Core Decodable 68

Bothell, WA • Chicago, IL • Columbus, OH • New York, NY

MHEonline.com

Mc Graw Hill Education

Send all inquiries to:
McGraw-Hill Education
8787 Orion Place
Columbus, OH 43240

At last, Hugo made music for Muse.

Muse did not like branches on his back.

Muse did not budge.

Muse is a cute mule.

Muse had a forest home.

Muse liked the forest.

But Muse liked music the most.

Hugo cut branches and traded them.

Muse had to lug the branches on his back.

"A live mule is stubborn."

"A robot mule is also stubborn."

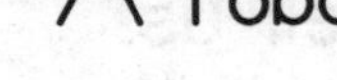

A Better Mule

by Tom Sato
illustrated by Rusty Fletcher

Core Decodable 69

Mc Graw Hill Education

Bothell, WA • Chicago, IL • Columbus, OH • New York, NY

MHEonline.com

Mc Graw Hill Education

Send all inquiries to:
McGraw-Hill Education
8787 Orion Place
Columbus, OH 43240

What is the problem?
Doctor Hugo will tell us.

Doctor Hugo and Rose check it.

The robot unit is not broken.

This is Doctor Hugo.

And this is Rose, a pupil.

They make robots.
They made a robot mule.
What for?

A fuse is not the problem.
Is this robot unit broken?

Fuel is not the problem.

Is it a fuse?

Rose opens the unit.

A live mule is cute.

Will it do what humans tell it?

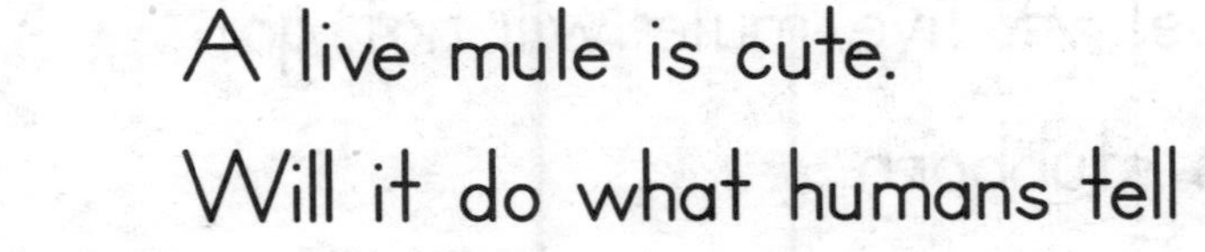

"Go!"

Nope! A live mule will not go!

It is stubborn.

Doctor Hugo is checking the fuel.

Is fuel the problem?

"Go! Go!"

There is a problem.

The mule will not go.

This is Doctor Hugo's mule.

It is not cute.

Is this robot mule stubborn?

Will it do what humans tell it?

We will have a test.

Rose will talk to the robot mule.

For the time being, we cannot tell.

Can you spot a zebra?

A Zebra

by Ethan Cruz
illustrated by Rusty Fletcher

Core Decodable 70

McGraw Hill Education

Bothell, WA • Chicago, IL • Columbus, OH • New York, NY

MHEonline.com

McGraw Hill Education

Send all inquiries to:
McGraw-Hill Education
8787 Orion Place
Columbus, OH 43240

So has the zebra left?
Or is he just well hidden?

We looked and looked all over.

But we did not even get a hint.

We made a recent visit to a ranch.

We visited these horses.

These horses have a big secret.
A zebra runs with them.

But which is the zebra?
These horses will not tell.

"Mom, the beach is neat," Jean calls.

"I agree," adds Dean.

Summer Heat

by Frederick Prugh
illustrated by Kristen Goeters

Core Decodable 71

Bothell, WA • Chicago, IL • Columbus, OH • New York, NY

MHEonline.com

McGraw Hill Education

Send all inquiries to:
McGraw-Hill Education
8787 Orion Place
Columbus, OH 43240

Jean sticks her two feet in the sea.
Dean feels the sea breeze.

Jean and Dean reach the beach.

The two kids see and smell the sea.

It will be a hot two weeks.

Jean and Dean feel the heat.

"Time for the beach you two?" asks Mom.

"Yes!" yell Jean and Dean.

Cars fill the streets.

They drive east to the beach.

The trip is over.

But it was so exciting!

Green River

by Joaquin Garcia
illustrated by Lyle Miller

Core Decodable 72

McGraw Hill Education

Bothell, WA • Chicago, IL • Columbus, OH • New York, NY

MHEonline.com

McGraw Hill Education

Send all inquiries to:
McGraw-Hill Education
8787 Orion Place
Columbus, OH 43240

At last, the river is not so fast.
Each kid takes a deep breath.

Rocks seem to pop up!
The rafts speed past them.

These kids will take a trip.
It will be down Green River.

Lee leads rafting trips.
She has a team.
Her team keeps kids safe.

The rafts go faster.
Green River has little, white bubbles.

The rafts leap up and down.
Kids smile. Kids scream.

Each kid needs a life jacket.
Kids even need helmets.

The kids and team have three rafts.
The kids sit on raft seats.

The kids paddle hard and deep.
The river splashes faces.

Then the river is between steep cliffs.

The rafts go faster.

At first, the trip is not fast.

Kids see fish in the clean river.

Kids paddle past big rocks and green trees.

The sun shines on Green River.

Lee looks up.

She spots an eagle.

The kids see it.

The party is over.

Happy puppies help clean up.

"Thanks for the help," Billy mutters.

A Party for Puppies

by Anne O'Brien
illustrated by Olivia Cole

Core Decodable 73

Bothell, WA • Chicago, IL • Columbus, OH • New York, NY

MHEonline.com

Mc Graw Hill Education

Send all inquiries to:
McGraw-Hill Education
8787 Orion Place
Columbus, OH 43240

Nellie gets more yummy treats.
"No more help, please!" yells Nellie.

Nellie has garden treats.
Billy places a treat on every plate.
Every puppy helps.

Nellie and Billy have fun parties.
They invite Nellie's babies and teddies.

Nellie gets a table. Billy sets the table.
Every puppy helps.

Nellie makes funny party hats.
Billy tapes ribbons on every hat.

"Dudley! Dudley! Are you going to help with the turkeys or not?"

Dudley the Donkey

by Rich Lewis
illustrated by Len Epstein

Core Decodable 74

Bothell, WA • Chicago, IL • Columbus, OH • New York, NY

MHEonline.com

Mc Graw Hill Education

Send all inquiries to:
McGraw-Hill Education
8787 Orion Place
Columbus, OH 43240

The fans will cheer, "Dudley! Dudley!"
The fans will toss me roses and carrots!

If I am the winner, I will get fame.
I will even get a key to the city.

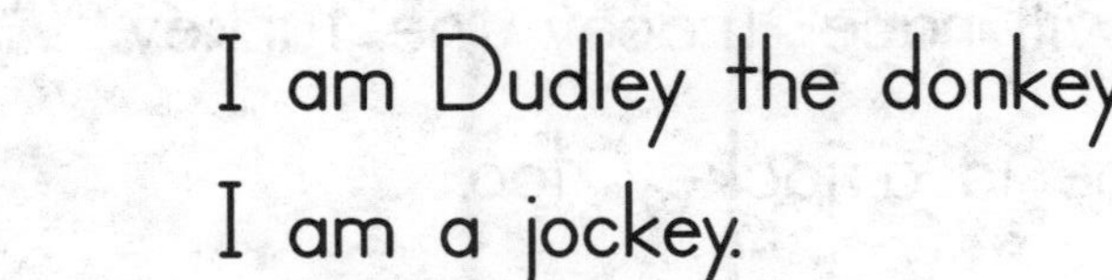

I am Dudley the donkey.
I am a jockey.

I will race Tracey the turkey.
She is a jockey, too.

Fans come to the valley to see the race.

Maggie opened a pretty box with green ribbon.
Maggie liked her gift.

Casey and Maggie

by Howard Lee
illustrated by Lorinda Cauley

Core Decodable 75

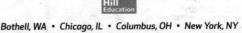

McGraw Hill Education

Bothell, WA • Chicago, IL • Columbus, OH • New York, NY

MHEonline.com

McGraw Hill Education

Send all inquiries to:
McGraw-Hill Education
8787 Orion Place
Columbus, OH 43240

These ideas helped Casey with her gift.
It seemed so easy.

Maggie liked the circus.

Here, Maggie was smiling at the funny man.

Casey's home was next to Maggie's.

Maggie was Casey's best buddy.

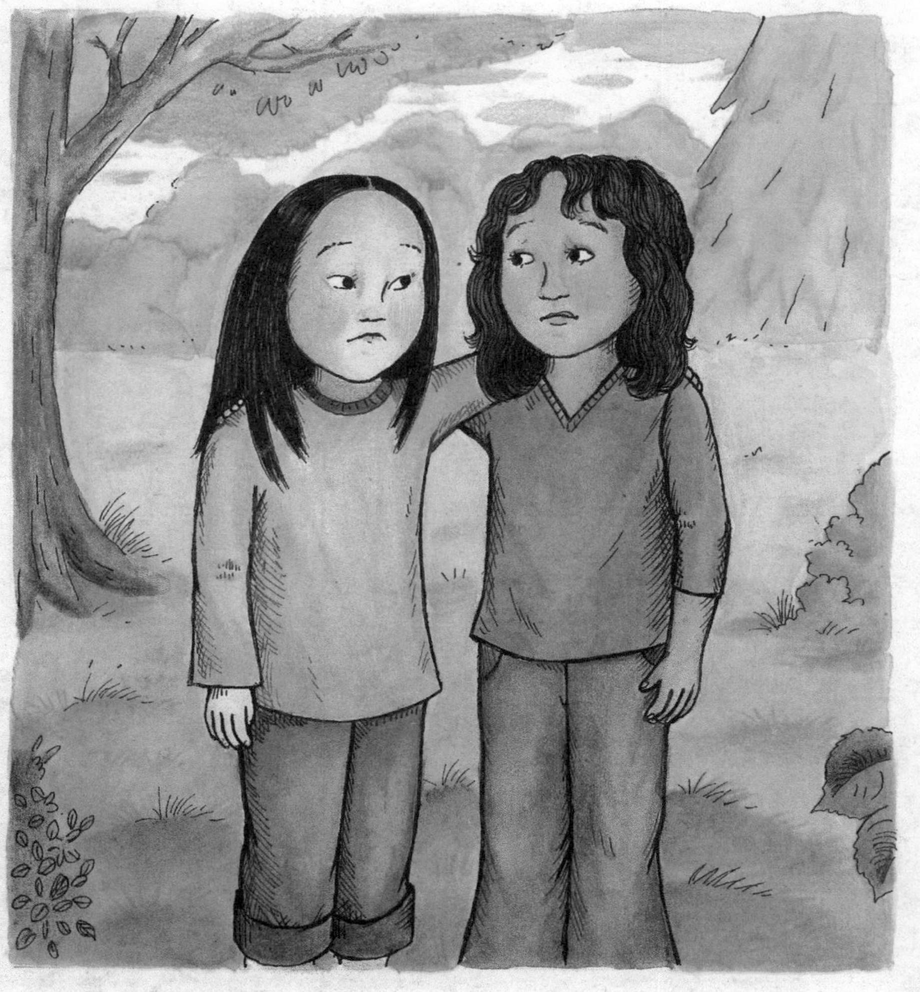

But Maggie had to go.
Her mom got a job in a big city.

Maggie liked to see homes go up.
She liked to see trucks on the street.

Maggie liked to skate on concrete.
Maggie skated fast, even with pads.

There was going to be a block party for Maggie's family.

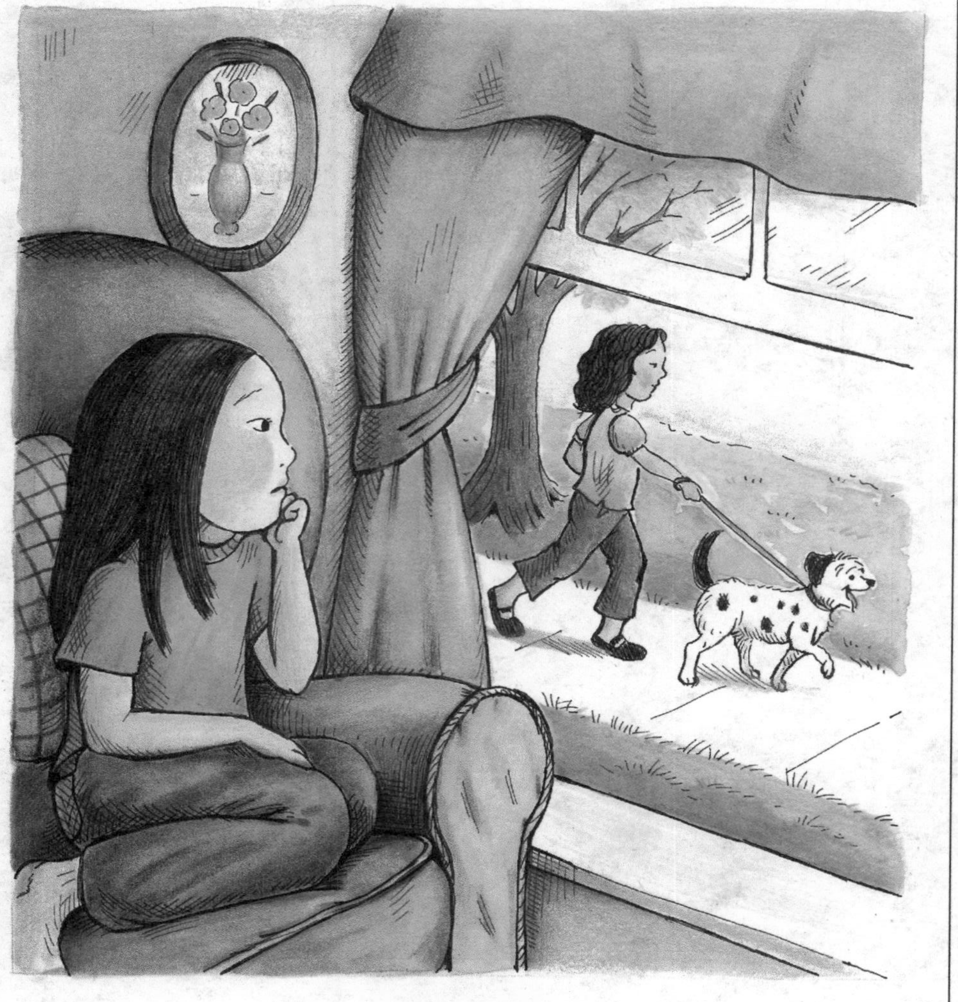

Casey was sad to see Maggie go.
She was going to miss Maggie.

Maggie sang on key.
Maggie danced to the beat.

Casey looked at Maggie.

It helped Casey think of memories.

Kids planned gifts for Maggie.

Some shopped for gifts.

Some made gifts.

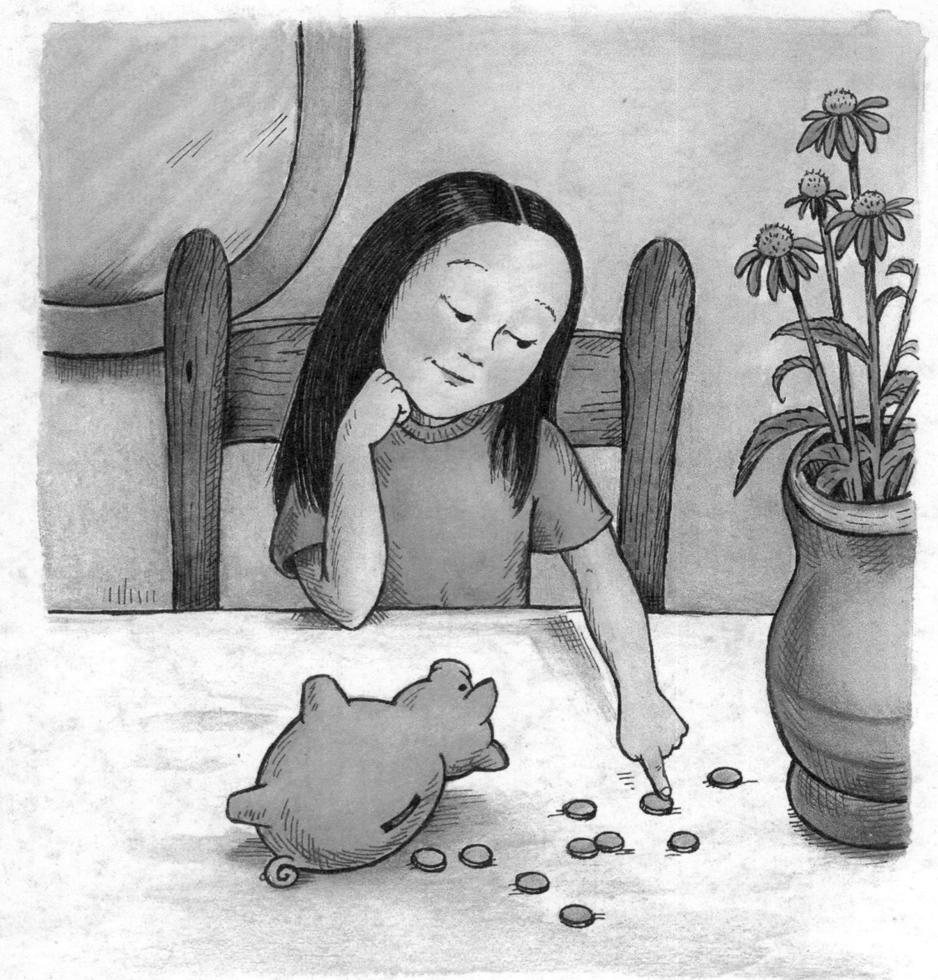

Casey could not shop for a gift.
She had only ten pennies in her piggy bank.

What could Casey create for Maggie?
Casey had to think.
What did Maggie like?

Mom made hot, spicy tea.
"I feel better," said Nancy.
"Hot, spicy tea is for winter."

A Fancy Jacket

by David Nguyen
illustrated by Susan Lexa

Core Decodable 76

Bothell, WA • Chicago, IL • Columbus, OH • New York, NY

MHEonline.com

McGraw Hill Education

Send all inquiries to:
McGraw-Hill Education
8787 Orion Place
Columbus, OH 43240

Nancy's teeth chattered.
"Yes, it is lacy," said Nancy.
"It isn't for winter."

Mom hugged Nancy.
"That fancy jacket is thin," Mom said.

Nancy's fancy jacket was thin.
She could feel the winter chill.

Nancy wished she could run.
But the sidewalk was icy.
She could fall.

Mom looked at Nancy.
She could tell Nancy was freezing.

"I will play," said Jay.

"I like to play when it is rainy and gray."

A Gray, Rainy Day

by Dennis Fertig
illustrated by Kersti Frigell

Core Decodable 77

Bothell, WA • Chicago, IL • Columbus, OH • New York, NY

MHEonline.com

McGraw Hill Education

Send all inquiries to:
McGraw-Hill Education
8787 Orion Place
Columbus, OH 43240

Kay went back to find Jay.
"It is gray and rainy!" said Kay.

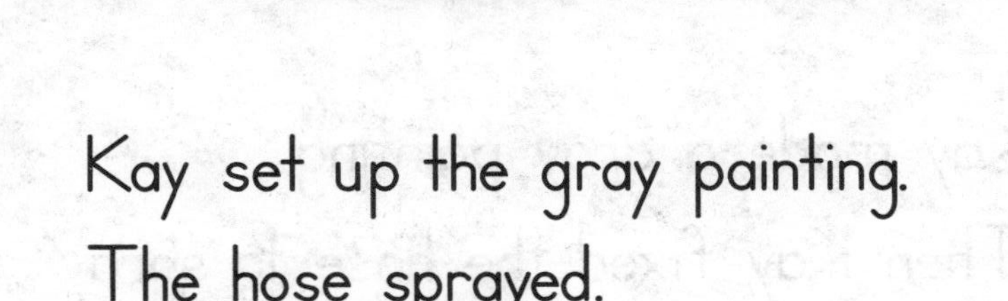

Kay set up the gray painting.
The hose sprayed.

"Will you play for us?" asked Kay.
"I will play on a gray, rainy day," said Jay.

Kay liked to hear Jay play.
Kay had a way to make Jay play.

Kay made a gray painting.
Then Kay fixed the hose to spray.

These kids skate all day.

Have you had a chance to skate?

Skating

by Martha Wood
illustrated by Diane Paterson

Core Decodable 78

Bothell, WA • Chicago, IL • Columbus, OH • New York, NY

MHEonline.com

Mc Graw Hill Education

Send all inquiries to:
McGraw-Hill Education
8787 Orion Place
Columbus, OH 43240

At some places, Gail races on ice.

At some places, Gail races on pavement.

Stay out of her way!

Since Ray was three, he has skated.
He sails down the pavement on skates.

Some kids skate on ice.
Some kids skate on pavement.

Kay takes lessons at City Center.
She always skates in fancy circles.

Aiden also ice skates.
His aim is to be fast, not fancy.

It is time for sleep.
The opossum stays with her babies.
They might play later at night.

The Opossum at Night

by Anne O'Brien
illustrated by Deborah Colvin Borgo

Core Decodable 79

Bothell, WA • Chicago, IL • Columbus, OH • New York, NY

MHEonline.com

Mc Graw Hill Education

Send all inquiries to:
McGraw-Hill Education
8787 Orion Place
Columbus, OH 43240

The opossum returns to her tree.
Her babies wait for her.

Night is over. It begins to get light.

Opossums do not like the light.

Daytime is bright.

An opossum sees better at night.

When it is night, an opossum wakes.
She hunts for insects to feed her babies.

A dog frightens the opossum.
The opossum freezes.
She stays still and plays dead.

"My head feels better in sand," explains Bly.

Why, Bly?

by Dottie Raymer
illustrated by Kersti Frigell

Core Decodable 80

Bothell, WA • Chicago, IL • Columbus, OH • New York, NY

MHEonline.com

McGraw Hill Education

Send all inquiries to:
McGraw-Hill Education
8787 Orion Place
Columbus, OH 43240

"Is Bly too shy?" asks a child.
"I am not too shy," Bly replies.

"Why not fly in the sky?" asks Eagle.
"I can't fly. I am too big," replies Bly.

Bly likes her head in dry sand.
Her pals don't understand why.

"Why not lie in the sun?" asks Snake.
"I get too hot in the sun," Bly replies.

"Why not hang in trees?" asks Chimp.
"I can't hang in trees," Bly replies.

That day, the kids raced.
Ray stayed with them.
It was a tie!

Wait for Me

by Sidney Allen
illustrated by Diane Paterson

Core Decodable 81

Bothell, WA • Chicago, IL • Columbus, OH • New York, NY

MHEonline.com

McGraw Hill Education

Send all inquiries to:
McGraw-Hill Education
8787 Orion Place
Columbus, OH 43240

Ray was riding alone.
"I am flying, Dad!" he yelled.

Ray pedaled fast.
Dad let the bike go.
Could Ray tell?

"Wait for me," called Ray.
But the kids were way ahead.

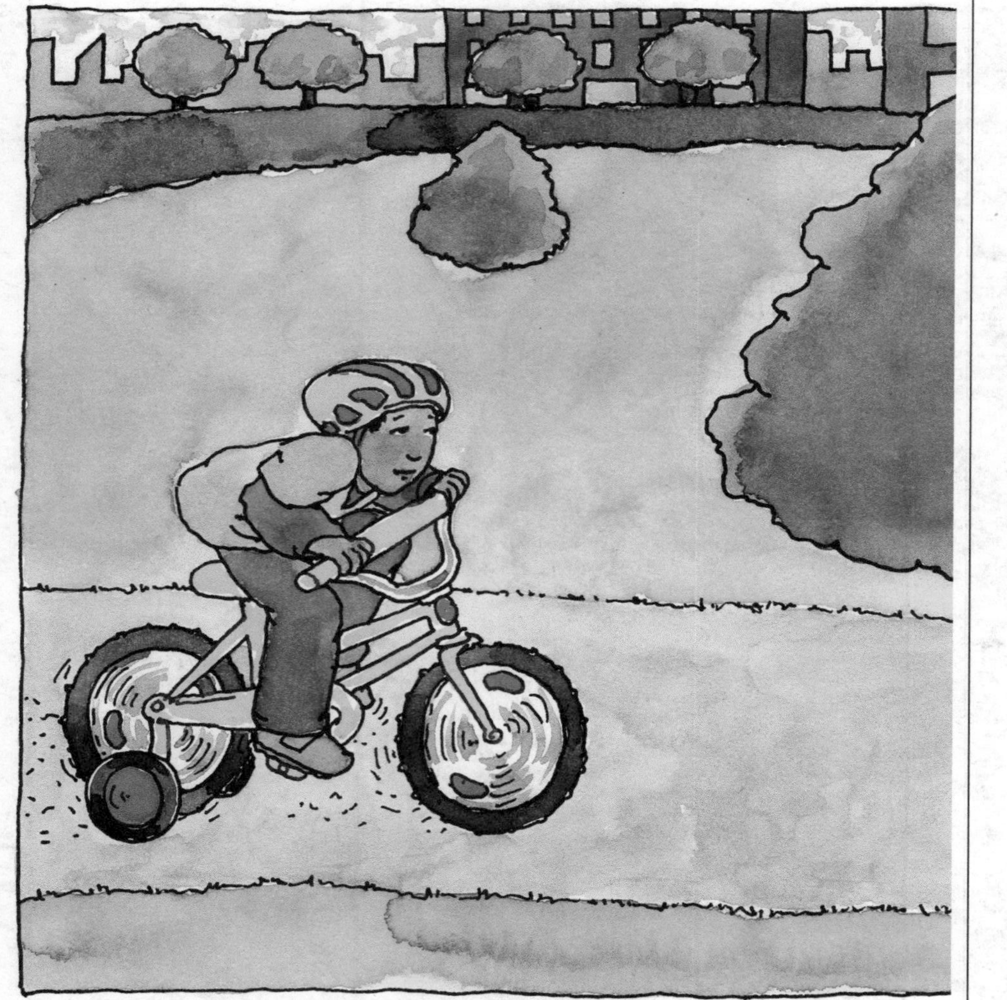

It was like this every day.
Ray kept trying.
But he could not keep up.

"Try riding this way," said Dad.
Dad held the bike as Ray pedaled.
Dad ran next to him.

Ray was glad.
But he was a little afraid.
He might need training wheels.

This time, the kids stopped on the corner.
But they came right back.

The kids passed Ray.
Ray turned his bike.
"Wait for me," he called.

Ray spotted his bike in the bright sun.
It did not have training wheels!

The next day, Dad called Ray.
"Go to the driveway," said Dad.

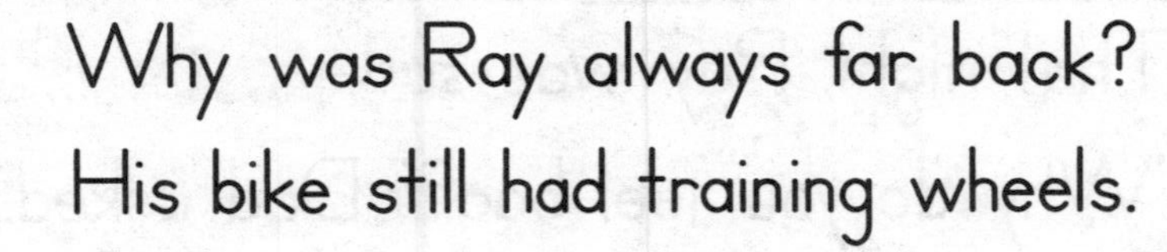

Why was Ray always far back?
His bike still had training wheels.

That night, Ray was sad.

"Why do you feel bad?" Dad asked.

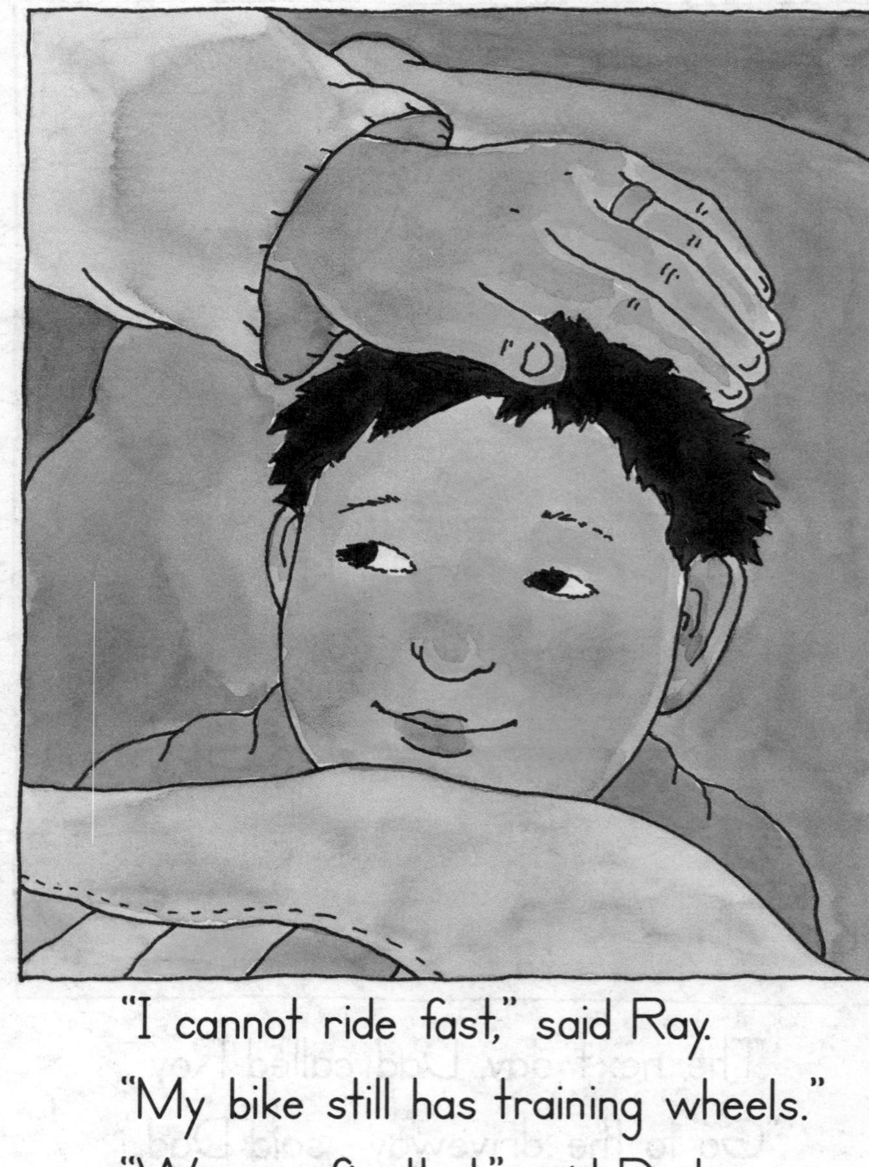

"I cannot ride fast," said Ray.

"My bike still has training wheels."

"We can fix that," said Dad.

"The boat has no sail!" yelled Toad.

"I think we must row," moaned Goat.

Crow and Goat

by Marilee Robin Burton
illustrated by Len Epstein

Core Decodable 82

McGraw Hill Education

Bothell, WA • Chicago, IL • Columbus, OH • New York, NY

MHEonline.com

Mc Graw Hill Education

Send all inquiries to:
McGraw-Hill Education
8787 Orion Place
Columbus, OH 43240

"This boat only floats," mumbled Crow. Goat groaned.

But the wind did not blow, and their boat did not go.

Their boat did not go fast or slow.

Crow and Goat went to their boat.

Crow and Goat hoped to see their pal Toad.

"Let's go fast, not slow!" said Goat.

"We will go fast in this boat!" boasted Crow.

"Let the wind blow!" bellowed Goat.

"Here we go!" yelled Crow.

Do not argue. We all value the cat.
She will rescue the cat. The cat mews.

Rescue That Cat!

by Linda Smith
illustrated by Kersti Frigell

Core Decodable 83

Bothell, WA • Chicago, IL • Columbus, OH • New York, NY

MHEonline.com

McGraw Hill Education

Send all inquiries to:
McGraw-Hill Education
8787 Orion Place
Columbus, OH 43240

Yes, let's not argue. Few value the cat like you.
You can rescue the cat.

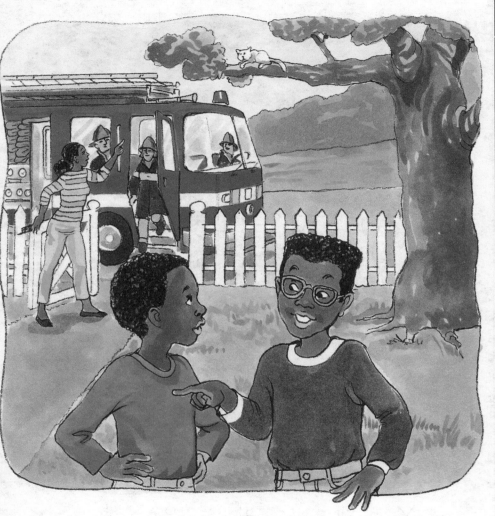

Let's not argue. We all value the cat.

You can rescue the cat.

A cat mews in a tree.

Will you rescue that cat?

The cat continues to mew.

I will rescue the cat.

You will rescue the cat?

No, I will rescue the cat.

Few like the cat as much as I do.

"Boat or not," I said.
"You must wait in line."
And they did.

Eat at Joan's

by Frederick Prugh
illustrated by Jane McCreary

Core Decodable 84

Mc Graw Hill Education
Bothell, WA • Chicago, IL • Columbus, OH • New York, NY

MHEonline.com

McGraw Hill Education

Send all inquiries to:
McGraw-Hill Education
8787 Orion Place
Columbus, OH 43240

But then I got it.
Fuel meant stuff to eat.
The men were hungry!

I was confused.
Sailboats do not need fuel.
Wind makes sailboats go.

My name is Joan.
I own this shop.
The shop is on the coast.

My shop is a drive-in.

Cars drive in and out.

Drivers get a meal at a value price.

The men talked to me.

"We need fuel," they said.

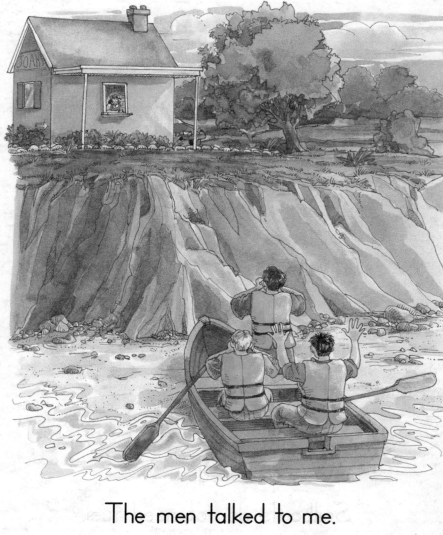

A rowboat left the boat.

Men rowed it to the coast.

I make a few yummy dishes.

I make my own veggie roast.

I make my own meatloaf.

The sun went down slowly.
I looked at the sea.
A lone boat sailed on the waves.

Still I could see the boat.
It was sailing to the coast.
Then it stopped.

I had to stay at the window.
I had to hand out dinners.
I had to do it fast.

A gentle wind was blowing.
The sailboat was not far away.

Lots of boats have passed this way.
But few have stopped.
Why did this boat sail closer?

But I could not look.
Lots of cars were in line.
They filled the road.

Dad can get Sam's lamb off the limb.
He did not even have to climb the tree!

A Lamb on a Limb

by Jan Stewart
illustrated by Pat Lucas-Morris

Core Decodable 85

Mc Graw Hill Education

Bothell, WA • Chicago, IL • Columbus, OH • New York, NY

MHEonline.com

Mc Graw Hill Education

Send all inquiries to:
McGraw-Hill Education
8787 Orion Place
Columbus, OH 43240

Thumbs and crumbs did not get Sam's lamb.
Sam's lamb is still on a limb.

I have crumbs from my sandwich.

Crumbs are no help to get Sam's lamb.

Is that Sam's stuffed lamb?

Yes! It is his lamb on that limb.

We can get Sam's lamb off the limb!
Let's think of a plan.

Can we grab the lamb with a thumb?
Can thumbs get Sam's lamb?

The knight packed a knapsack.
He went away happily.

King Knox and His Knight

by Joyce Mallery
illustrated by Len Epstein

Core Decodable 86

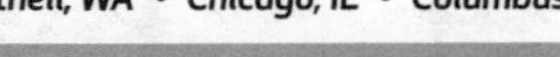

Bothell, WA • Chicago, IL • Columbus, OH • New York, NY

MHEonline.com

Mc Graw Hill Education

Send all inquiries to:
McGraw-Hill Education
8787 Orion Place
Columbus, OH 43240

The knight got down on his knee.
"I know I don't want to be a knight."

King Knox was getting mad. "You don't know much. What do you know?"

King Knox assigned things for his knight to do. "Tie some knots," he ordered.

"And sharpen this knife," King Knox ordered.

"I don't know how," replied his knight.

"I want you to knit socks," King Knox ordered.

"I don't know how," replied his knight.

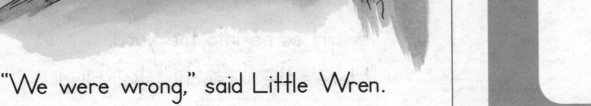

"We were wrong," said Little Wren.
"It is a thing to fix bikes!"

Little Wren's Surprise

by Joyce Mallery
illustrated by Deborah Colvin Borgo

Core Decodable 87

Bothell, WA • Chicago, IL • Columbus, OH • New York, NY

MHEonline.com

McGraw Hill Education

Send all inquiries to:
McGraw-Hill Education
8787 Orion Place
Columbus, OH 43240

A girl came into the yard.
"Here's the wrench!" she yelled.
"Now we can fix my bike."

"Let's wrap it up," said Little Wren.
But the wrinkled paper was too small.

One day, a wren family saw
a strange thing on the grass.

"What is it?" asked Dad.

He tried wriggling under it, but it was too big.

"Can you write with it?" asked Mom.

Mom rubbed it. It made no marks.

Peep, peep, peep.

"I see the phantom. It's the little frog,"

Ralph tells Phillip.

The Phantom Frog

by Irene Belnik

illustrated by Kersti Frigell

Core Decodable 88

Bothell, WA • Chicago, IL • Columbus, OH • New York, NY

MHEonline.com

McGraw-Hill Education

Send all inquiries to:
McGraw-Hill Education
8787 Orion Place
Columbus, OH 43240

Phillip looks for phantoms.

Ralph whispers, "Wait. Let me take a photo of this frog."

"Don't be silly!" scolds Ralph. "Phantoms are phony."

Peep, peep, peep.

"Then what is it?" asks Phillip.

Phillip and Ralph take a hike.

They left their cell phones at home.

Phillip finds leaves like elephant ears.
Ralph takes photographs of birds.

Peep, peep, peep.
"Think that's a gopher?" asks Ralph.
Phillip whispers, "Maybe it's a phantom!"

Would Tony get the wrench to Mom?

Yes! He was the Tony Express!

The Pony Express

by Phillip Wright
illustrated by Audrey Durney

Core Decodable 89

Mc Graw Hill Education

Bothell, WA • Chicago, IL • Columbus, OH • New York, NY

MHEonline.com

Mc Graw Hill Education

Send all inquiries to:
McGraw-Hill Education
8787 Orion Place
Columbus, OH 43240

The note said, "Please lend me a wrench!" Gramps grinned. "Thank you, rider," he said.

Tony knocked twice. Knock, knock. "I am the Tony Express! I have mail," said Tony.

Tony looked at photos. "What was the Pony Express?" he asked Mom.

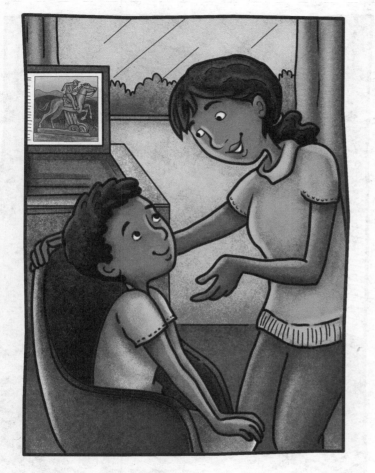

Mom smiled. "In old times, riders on horses would take mail from place to place. That was the Pony Express."

Tony's horse was strong. A wrong step might mean a bad fall.

The Tony Express started his ride. He climbed down high steps.

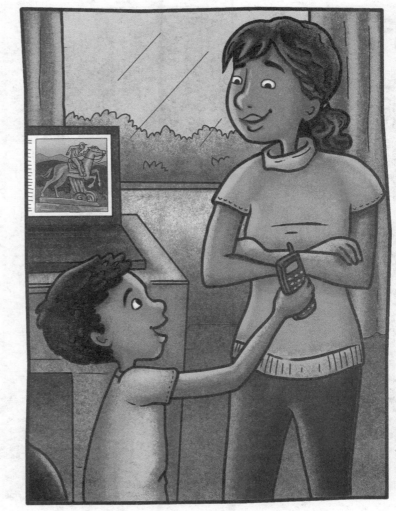

"I would just use a phone!" said Tony.

"There were no phones back then," said Mom.

"Pony Express riders rode fast. Few riders could do it," Mom explained.

"Look out for gopher holes and tree limbs!" Mom yelled.

Mom wrote a note. "Can the Tony Express take this to Gramps?" she asked. Tony nodded.

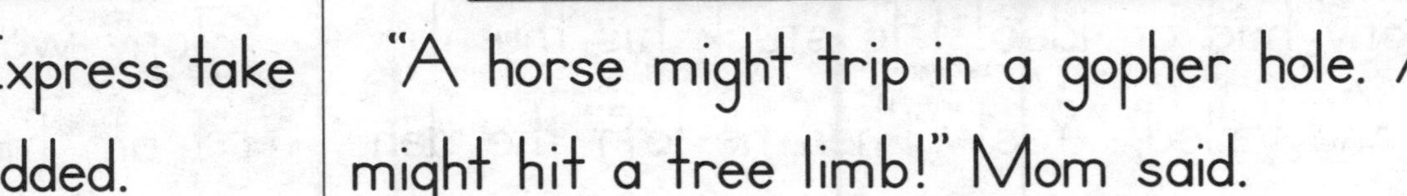

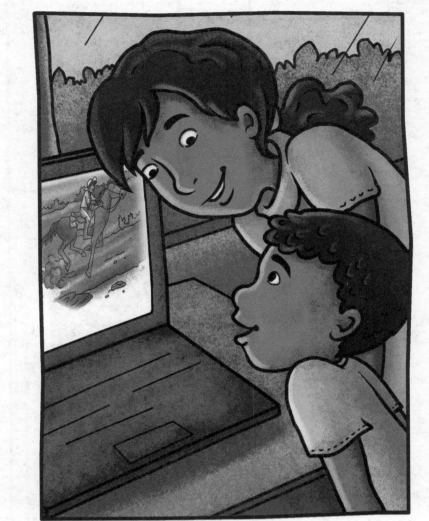

"A horse might trip in a gopher hole. A rider might hit a tree limb!" Mom said.

Tony had an idea! He stuck his thumb up and yelled, "Yes!" Then he left the den.

Tony was back. He had an old hat. "I am the Tony Express!" he said. Mom smiled.

A first grader looked at the balloon.
It looked like a floating apple.
"Cool," she said.

A Cool Balloon

by Alex Yu
illustrated by Alex Wallner

Core Decodable 90

Bothell, WA • Chicago, IL • Columbus, OH • New York, NY

MHEonline.com

McGraw Hill Education

Send all inquiries to:
McGraw-Hill Education
8787 Orion Place
Columbus, OH 43240

The riders spotted a goose flying below.
They could see a jet zoom high over them.

The ride was smooth.

The balloon drifted for miles.

Riders could see for miles, too.

At first, the balloon just drooped.

But it pumped up fast.

Soon it was filled and ready.

Riders climbed in the basket.

A man set the balloon loose.

The balloon floated higher and higher.

It passed over roofs.

"Cool!" said a rider.

"I see the truth!" yelled Sue.

"It's hard to fool you, Sue," Ruth said.

A True Bird

by Maria Johnson
illustrated by Lorinda Cauley

Core Decodable 91

Mc Graw Hill Education
Bothell, WA • Chicago, IL • Columbus, OH • New York, NY

MHEonline.com

Mc Graw Hill Education

Send all inquiries to:
McGraw-Hill Education
8787 Orion Place
Columbus, OH 43240

Ruth had glued a paper bird on the stick.
It was not a true bird.

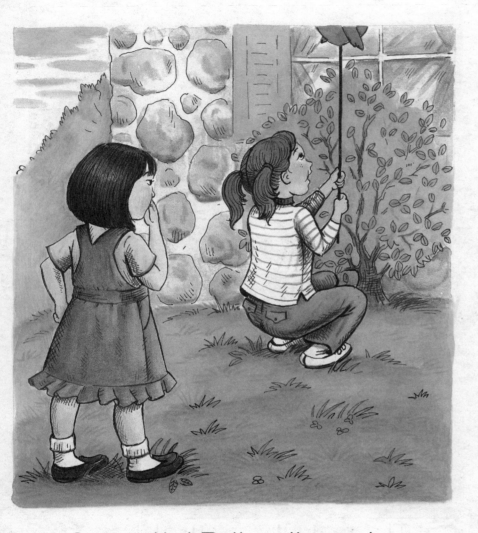

Sue spotted Ruth in the yard.

Ruth had a stick.

Sue spotted a bird.

What kind was it?

She did not have one clue.

The bird had one blue wing.
It had one ruby red wing.
Birds don't have wings like that!

And birds fly.
This one just jumped a bit.
"Is this a true bird?" asked Sue.

So this is the real story.
It is all true.
Ants fool humans.

Ants: The True Story

by Robert Bridges
illustrated by John Hovell

Core Decodable 92

Bothell, WA • Chicago, IL • Columbus, OH • New York, NY

MHEonline.com

Mc Graw Hill Education

Send all inquiries to:
McGraw-Hill Education
8787 Orion Place
Columbus, OH 43240

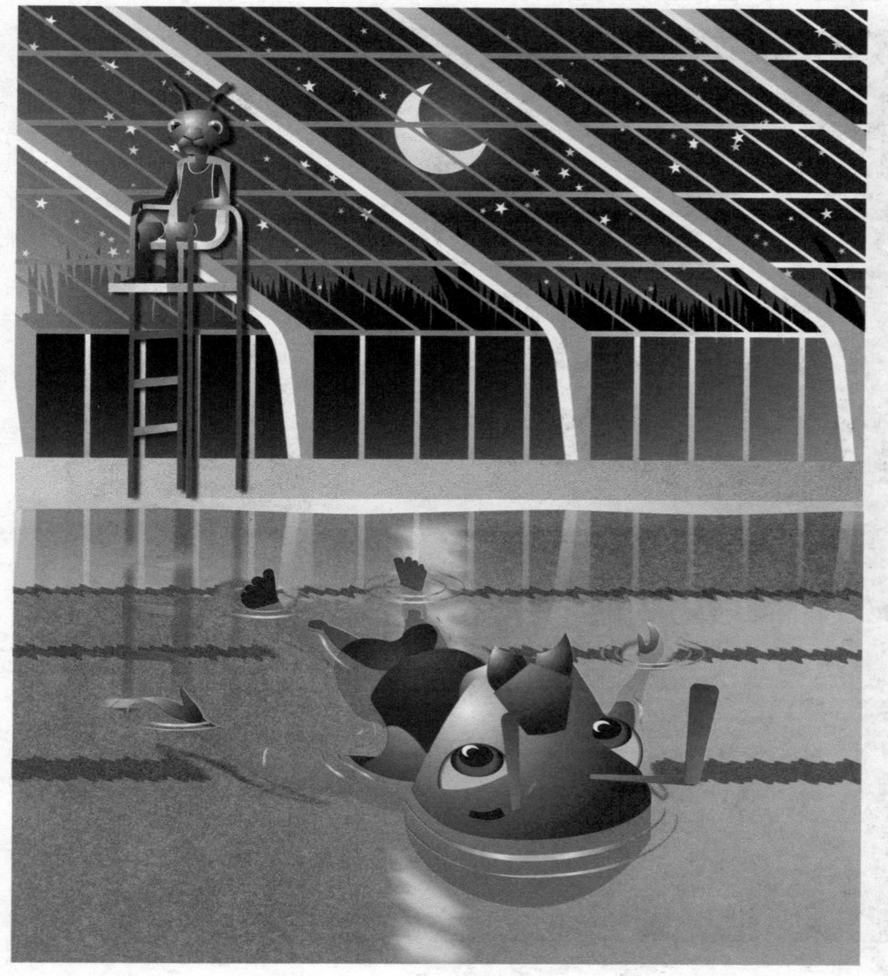

I can float on my back.

I can see the moon.

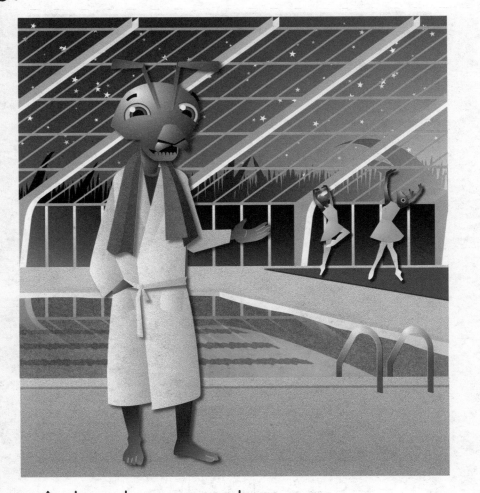

Ants get exercise, too.

We swim in a pool under a glass roof.

Some ants dance in tutus.

Ants fool humans.

Humans think we just dig nests.

They think we dig like bugs.

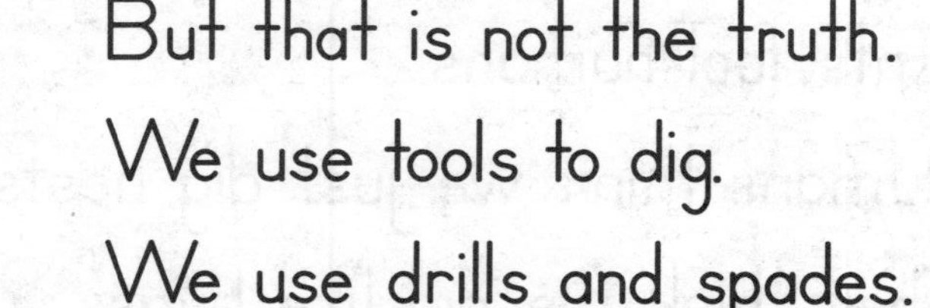

But that is not the truth.
We use tools to dig.
We use drills and spades.

Some ants read.
Some read papers.
I am reading a story.

In the evening, ants rest.

Some hear music.

Two ants play a tuba duet.

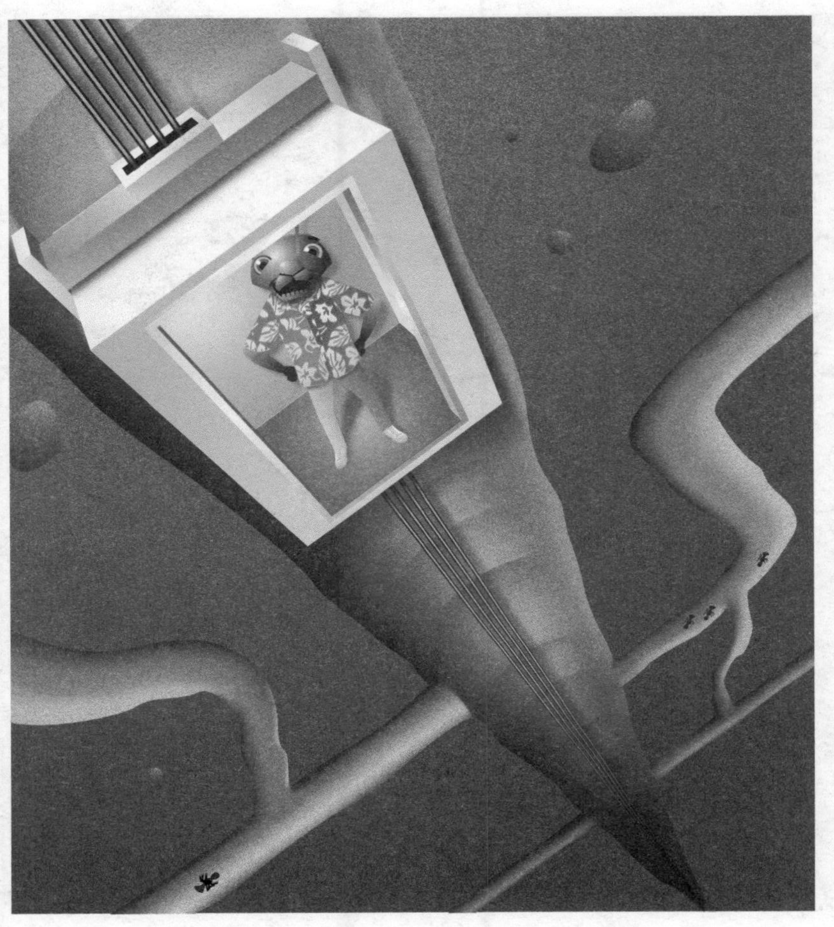

And ants do not walk down.

We zoom down in nests.

It is a fast, smooth ride.

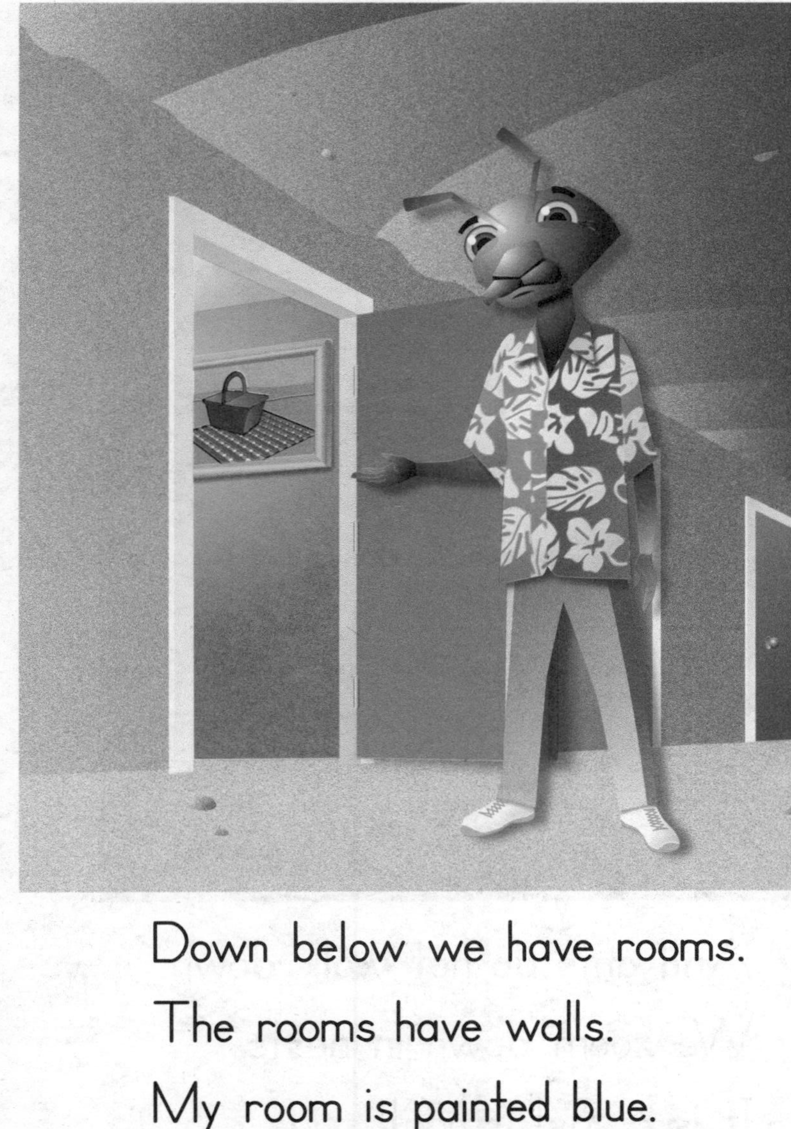

Down below we have rooms.
The rooms have walls.
My room is painted blue.

After we eat, we clean up.
Ants must do their duty.
I use a broom.

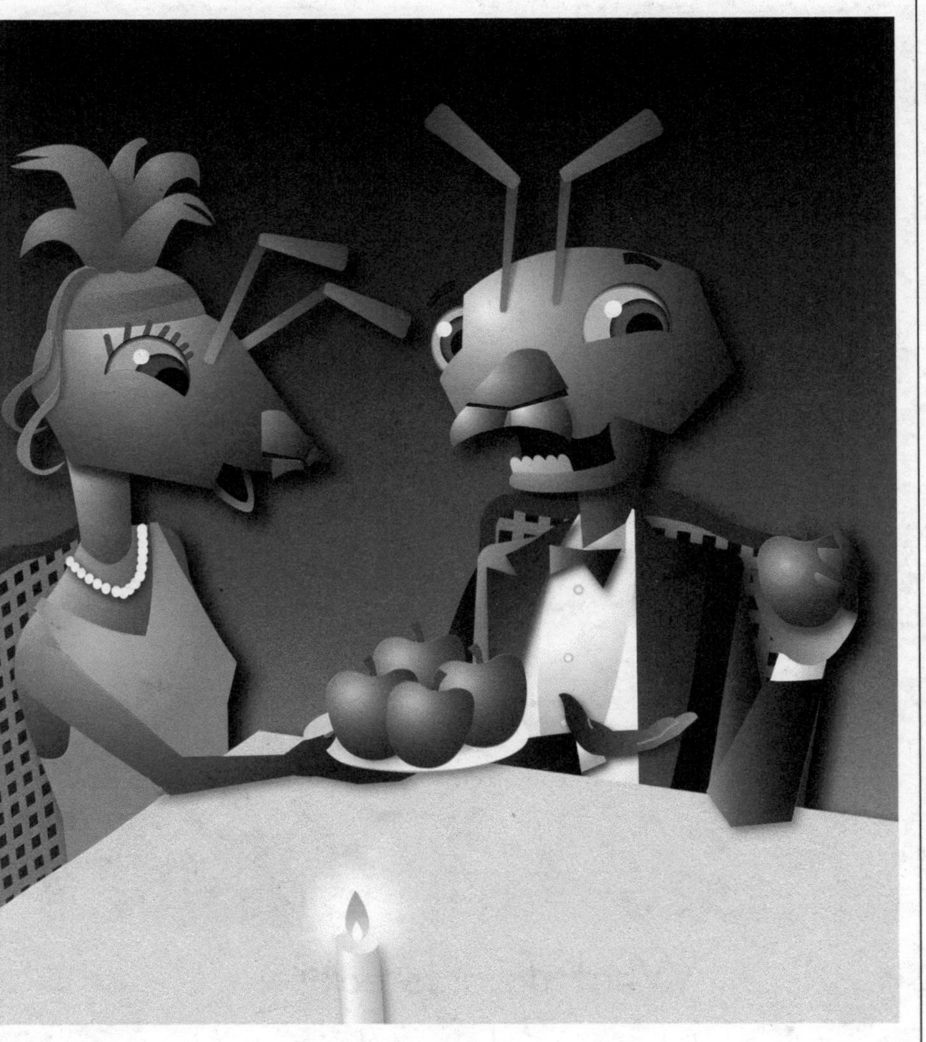

Do ants like sweets?

We do, but we eat healthy food, too.

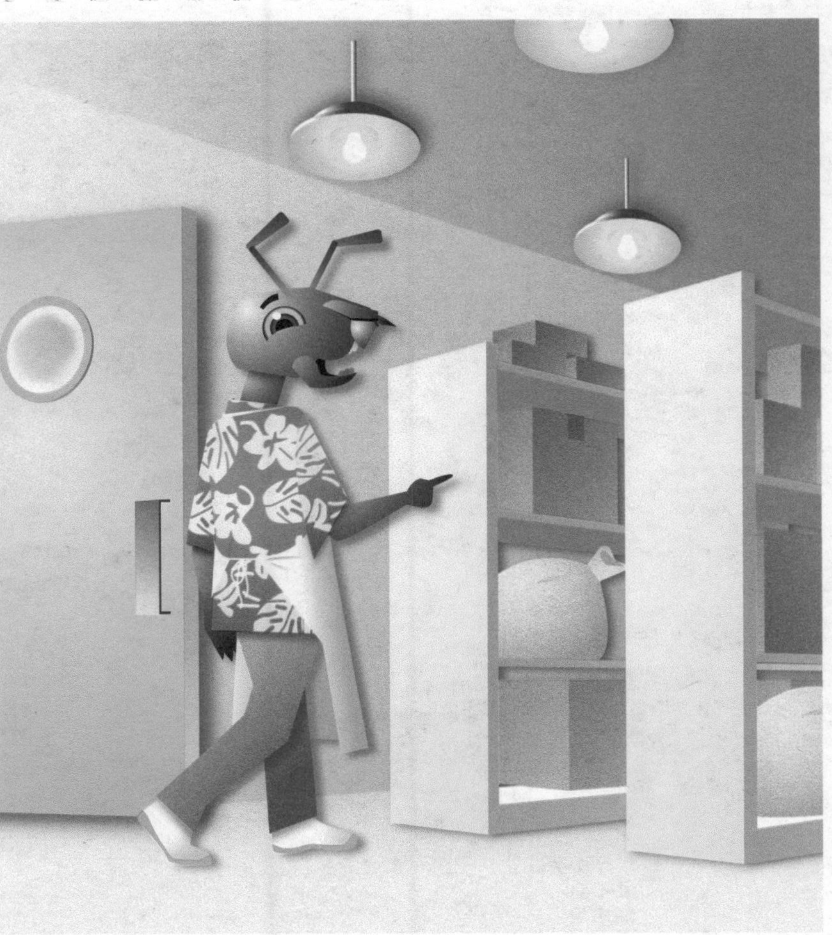

Humans think we store food.

Well, we truly do.

But not the way humans think.

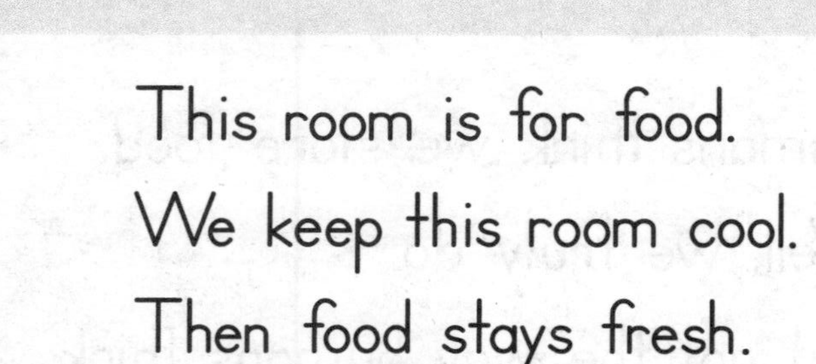

This room is for food.
We keep this room cool.
Then food stays fresh.

What do ants eat?
Humans do not have a clue!
Ants eat the best food.

Drew had his flute.

Drew played the new tune.

He played the tune very well!

A New Tune

by Charles Broderick

illustrated by Lyle Miller

Core Decodable 93

Bothell, WA • Chicago, IL • Columbus, OH • New York, NY

MHEonline.com

Mc Graw Hill Education

Send all inquiries to:
McGraw-Hill Education
8787 Orion Place
Columbus, OH 43240

It was a very hot summer day.
Flags flew high.
It was time for Drew to play.

Drew's fingers hurt!

But he still played his flute.

He played every day in June.

Drew played his flute.

He played in his room every day.

Drew played a new tune.

The new tune was very hard.

He did not play it very well.

Drew played and played the tune.

He blew and blew.

Drew had to get it right.

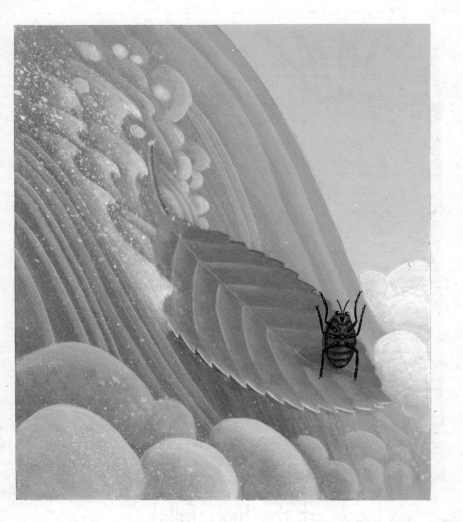

The bug rode down the falls!
"I took a good ride!" she said.

A Good Ride

by Andrea Patel
illustrated by Tom Leonard

Core Decodable 94

McGraw Hill Education
Bothell, WA • Chicago, IL • Columbus, OH • New York, NY

MHEonline.com

McGraw Hill Education

Send all inquiries to:
McGraw-Hill Education
8787 Orion Place
Columbus, OH 43240

Look at the high falls!
"I am afraid," the bug called.
Now she shook and shook.

The stream took a sharp turn.
Now it was a fast river.
The leaf shook.

A bug jumped on a leaf in a brook.
"Now I will take a ride," she said.

The bug had a foot in the brook.
She looked ahead.

The brook was now a quick stream.
"This is a good ride," said the bug.
She stood up.

"A camping trip?" asked Luke.

"Yes," said Mom. "You can make a book, too."

Mom's Book

by Cecilia Winters
illustrated by Susan Lexa

Core Decodable 95

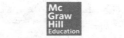

Mc Graw Hill Education
Bothell, WA • Chicago, IL • Columbus, OH • New York, NY

MHEonline.com

Mc Graw Hill Education

Send all inquiries to:
McGraw-Hill Education
8787 Orion Place
Columbus, OH 43240

The book had blank pages.

"You can fill those on a trip this June," said Mom.

Just then Dad walked in. He had a new book.

"This is for you, Luke," said Dad.

Mom looked at a book.

"Is that book good?" asked Luke.

Mom smiled.

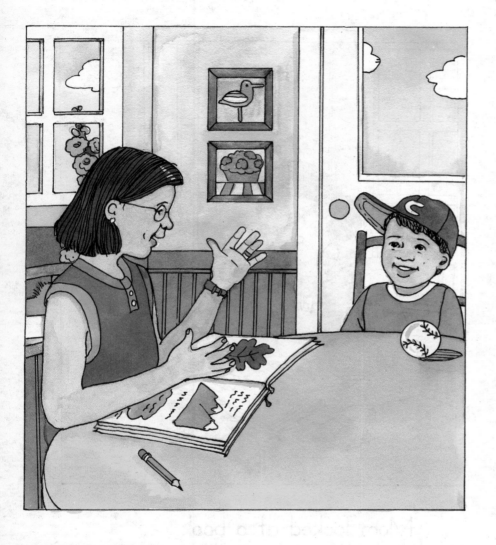

"I like it," said Mom. "The truth is I made it."

"You did?" asked Luke.

"Yes," said Mom. "There is the proof."

A snapshot was glued to a page.

"The trip was fun," said Mom. "I even spotted a moose."

"A moose!" said Luke.

"When I was a girl," said Mom, "I was on a trip. This book tells what I did."

"I went camping," said Mom. "I was with my mom and dad. We took a van."

"I threw in too much salt. Three big spoons," Mom said.

Her grin grew bigger.

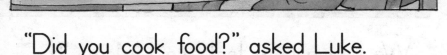

"Did you cook food?" asked Luke.

"Yes," Mom grinned. "I made bad stew!"

Mom showed Luke a page.

"I drew a map," said Mom. "It shows the way."

"The trip was in June," said Mom. "I said that it was hot. But it was cool at night."

"We had a new tent," said Mom. "It was dark blue. I drew that, too."

The Browns took the bus out of town.
On the way home, Howie said, "Wow!
Clowns are much better than rain showers."

A Clown in Town

by Dina McClellan
illustrated by Len Epstein

Core Decodable 96

Bothell, WA • Chicago, IL • Columbus, OH • New York, NY

MHEonline.com

Send all inquiries to:
McGraw-Hill Education
8787 Orion Place
Columbus, OH 43240

Chowder the Clown did tricks. He made a cat bark and a dog meow.

It was hot and crowded, but the Browns did not care.

Rain showers are good for flowers, but not for the Brown family. The Browns were tired of being inside.

"How can we see clowns?" asked Howie.

"Is the circus in town?" asked Dad.

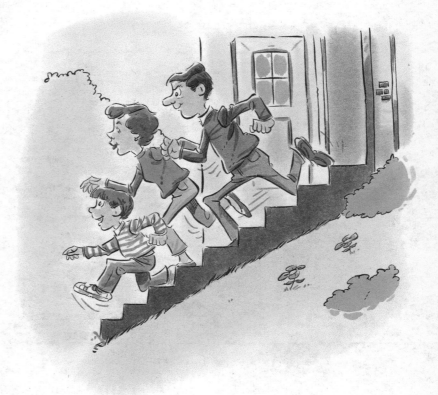

"Yes! There are clowns at the circus in town," said Mom.

The Browns ran down the stairs and rode the bus to town.

Pat went to feed Max.

"Look, Mom!" Pat whispered.

"Max found a mouse pal!"

Max was finally happy.

Max the Grouch

by Joyce Mallery
illustrated by Len Epstein

Core Decodable 97

Bothell, WA • Chicago, IL • Columbus, OH • New York, NY

MHEonline.com

Mc Graw Hill Education

Send all inquiries to:
McGraw-Hill Education
8787 Orion Place
Columbus, OH 43240

"How about a long walk?" asked Pat.
She and Max walked around the park.
Now Max was a tired grouch.

Max spit the bone out of his mouth.
He made a loud sound!
Max was still a grouch.

Pat hugged her hound, Max.
But Max was a grouch!
What will make Max happy?

"Maybe Max needs a new doghouse," said Mom.
But Max was still a grouch.

"How about a pound of dog bones?" asked Dad.

Dad set a large bone on the ground.

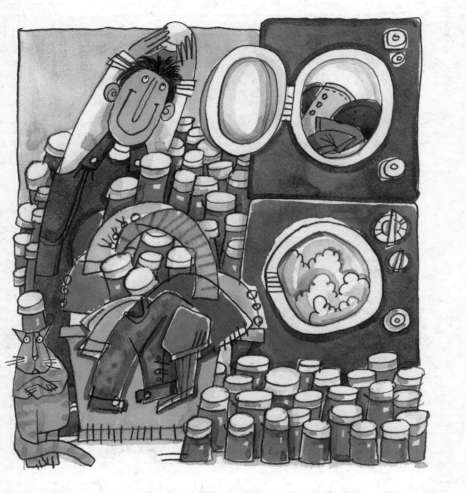

Paul makes jars and jars of sauce. I saw them in his basement and in his laundry.

Paul, stop making sauce!

Paul's Sauce

by Howard Lee
illustrated by Liz Callen

Core Decodable 98

Bothell, WA • Chicago, IL • Columbus, OH • New York, NY

MHEonline.com

Send all inquiries to:
McGraw-Hill Education
8787 Orion Place
Columbus, OH 43240

Paul mixes his sauce with straw for the cows. Paul's cat gets saucers of sauce. The cat has sauce on its paws!

But Paul mixes sauce with cereal and raw beets. That tastes awful!

Paul likes to cook. He makes sauce. Because he likes it, he makes a lot.

Paul starts at dawn. He makes sauce all day. He yawns at night. But he still makes sauce.

Paul uses sauce a lot. He mixes it with noodles and meat. That is fine.

Gramps smiled and gave it back.

"No thanks, Paul," said Gramps.

Gramps felt even prouder of Paul.

Foul Ball!

by Joaquin Garcia
illustrated by Lyle Miller

Core Decodable 99

Mc Graw Hill Education

Bothell, WA • Chicago, IL • Columbus, OH • New York, NY

MHEonline.com

McGraw Hill Education

Send all inquiries to:
McGraw-Hill Education
8787 Orion Place
Columbus, OH 43240

Paul held the round ball for a second. Then he gave it to Gramps.

"This ball is for you, Gramps," said Paul.

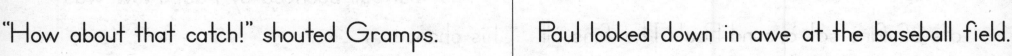

"How about that catch!" shouted Gramps. Paul looked at the ball. Paul looked at Gramps.

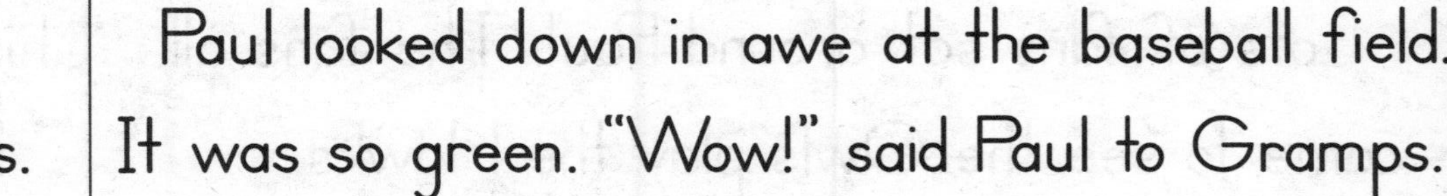

Paul looked down in awe at the baseball field. It was so green. "Wow!" said Paul to Gramps.

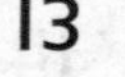

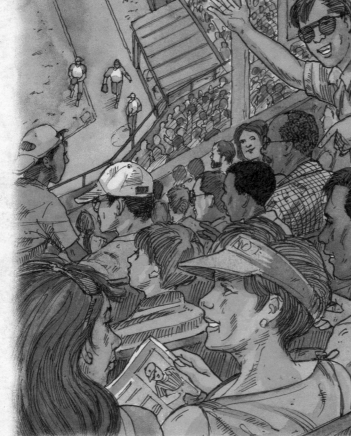

Lots of fans sat around Paul. The fans all came to see the Owls play the Hawks.

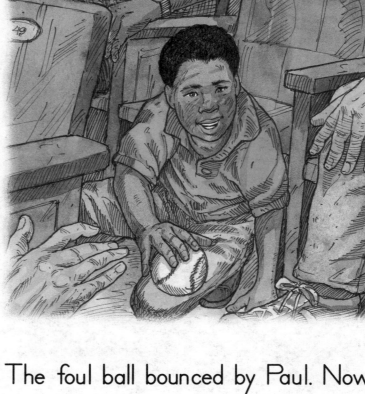

The foul ball bounced by Paul. Now was his chance.

Paul got the foul ball! Gramps felt proud.

But the ball did not reach them. Paul saw it hit a cement step. It made a loud sound as it bounced.

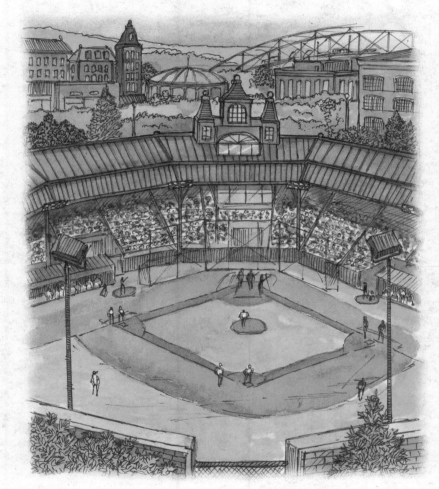

The Owls were the town's team. The Owls played at Brown Park.

Paul was thrilled because it was hard to get Owls tickets. But Gramps had found a way.

It was a high foul ball. The ball flew in the stands close to Paul and Gramps!

The best hitter was up. The pitch was fast. Pow! He launched the ball way up!

I like these seats," said Paul. "We could catch a foul ball."

"Maybe," said Gramps.

Gramps had seen lots of Owls games. But Gramps never got a foul ball.

Soon the game started. The crowd applauded. Fans squawked, "Go, Owls, go!"

The concert ended with applause.
"I am clapping for the music," he thought.
"And because I stayed awake!"

Mr. Daw Thought

by Frederick Prugh
illustrated by Nicole Rutten

Core Decodable 100

Mc Graw Hill Education

Bothell, WA • Chicago, IL • Columbus, OH • New York, NY

MHEonline.com

Mc Graw Hill Education

Send all inquiries to:
McGraw-Hill Education
8787 Orion Place
Columbus, OH 43240

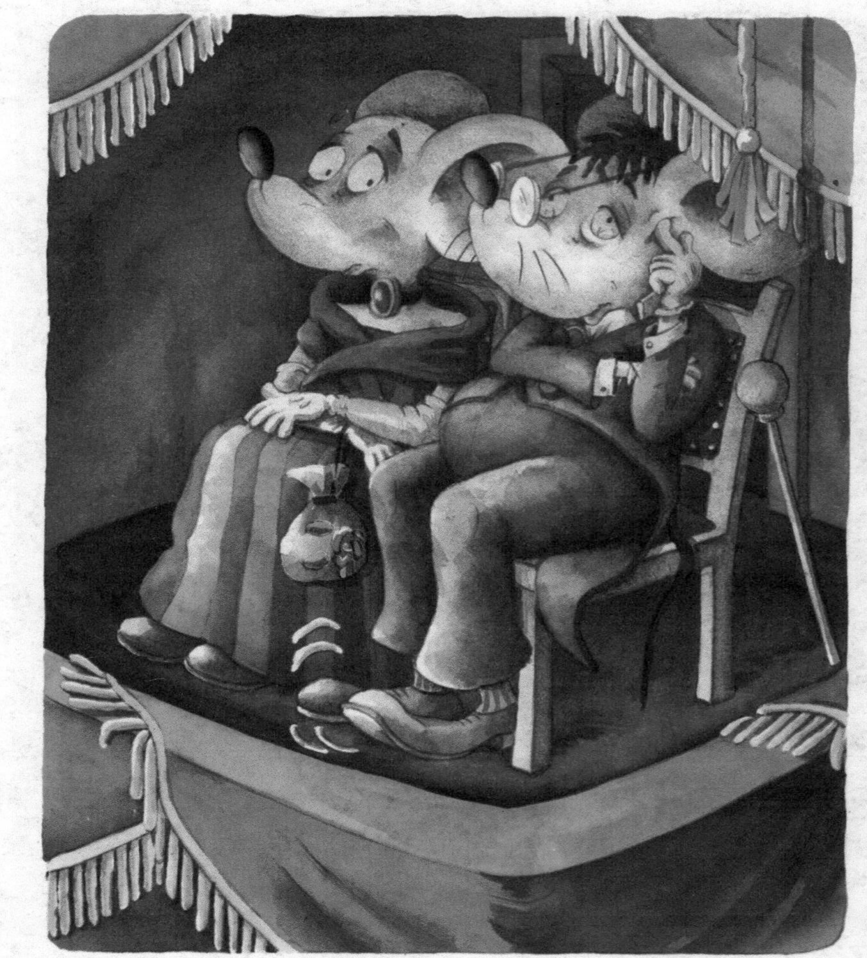

Mr. Daw started to tap his foot. "Tapping ought to keep me awake," he thought.

Mr. Daw started to doze. His daughter sneezed into a cloth. He awoke.

"Don't get caught sleeping!" he thought.

Mr. Daw was so tired. He brought heavy loads of cheese into his shop all day.

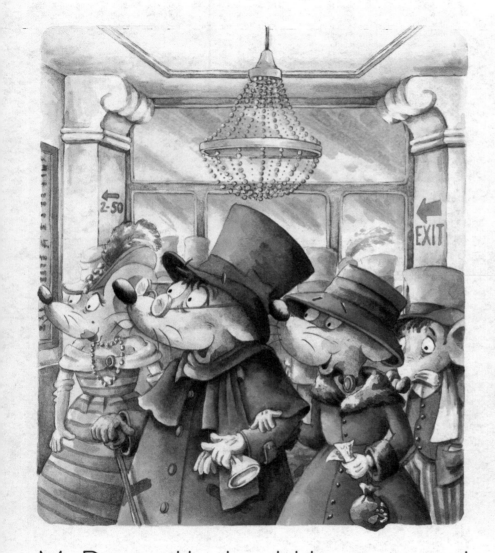

Mr. Daw could not rest. He was going into a concert hall. His daughter had bought tickets.

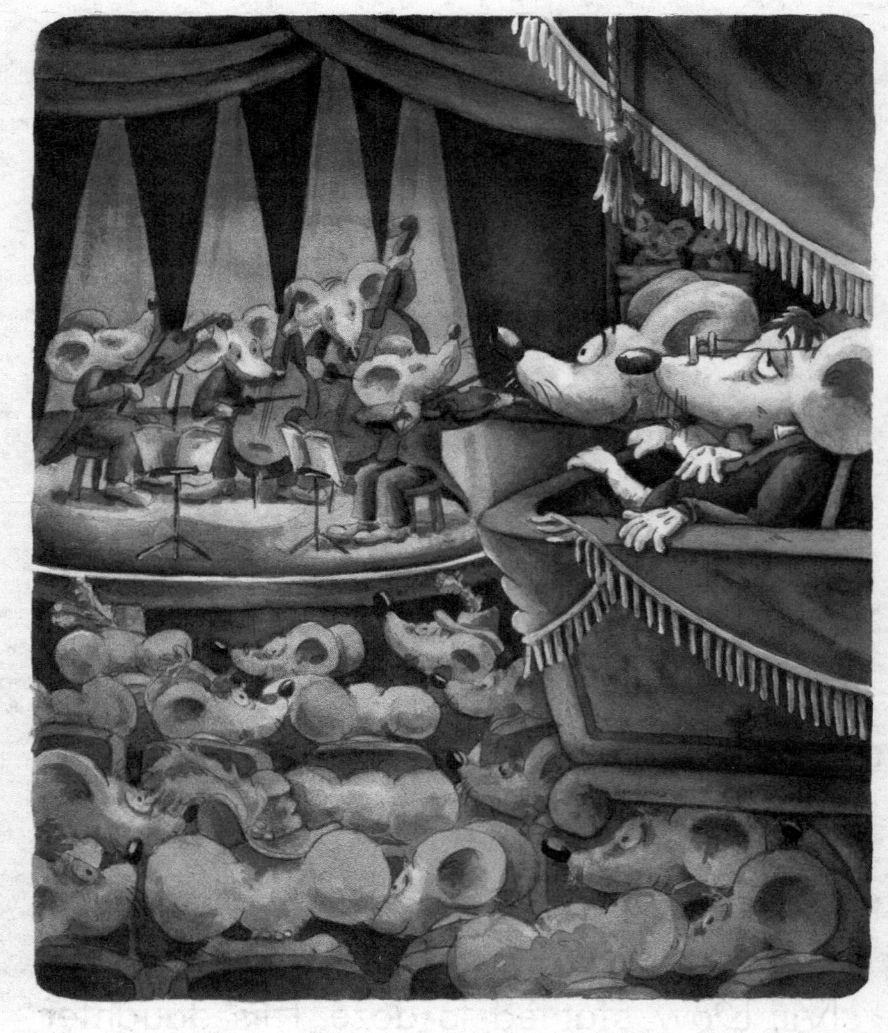

Mr. Daw liked music, but he was tired. He fought to stay awake as he sat into his seat.

Roy picked his beans. Royal dug up his bone. That night, the boy enjoyed a good dinner. Royal enjoyed his bone.

Roy and Royal

by Tom Sato
illustrated by Angela Adams

Core Decodable 101

McGraw Hill Education
Bothell, WA • Chicago, IL • Columbus, OH • New York, NY

MHEonline.com

Mc Graw Hill Education

Send all inquiries to:
McGraw-Hill Education
8787 Orion Place
Columbus, OH 43240

The green beans grew. Rabbits tried to destroy them. But Royal spoiled the rabbits' snack. He chased them away.

Roy felt joy. Green points stuck out of the soil. His green beans were growing.

Roy dug in the soil. His dog, Royal, joined him. Roy enjoyed gardening. Royal enjoyed digging.

Roy dropped seeds in the soil. He planted green beans. Royal planted a bone.

Roy used a hose. He kept the soil moist. Roy waited for the seeds to grow.

Then I saw a third bunting on my awning.

I was ready for fall.

At Dawn

by Natalie Lambert
illustrated by Kristin Goeters

Core Decodable 102

Bothell, WA • Chicago, IL • Columbus, OH • New York, NY

MHEonline.com

Mc Graw Hill Education

Send all inquiries to:
McGraw-Hill Education
8787 Orion Place
Columbus, OH 43240

I rejoiced as I drove home. But at home, I saw a second bunting on my lawn!

There sat a bright blue bunting! I was overjoyed! I saw it at last!

I bought a book about birds. I looked for birds shown in my book. I could not find one bird. It was the bunting.

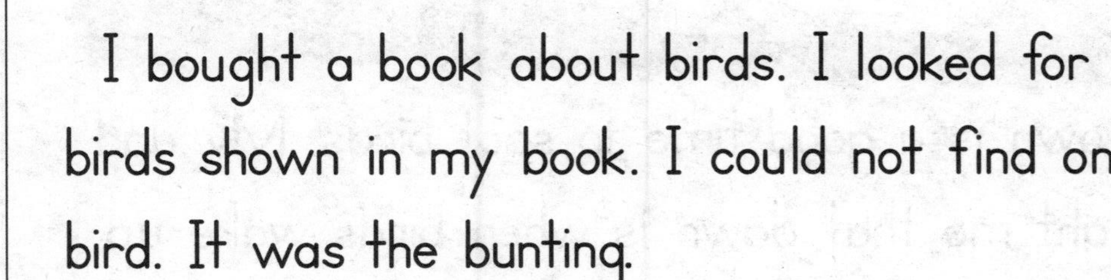

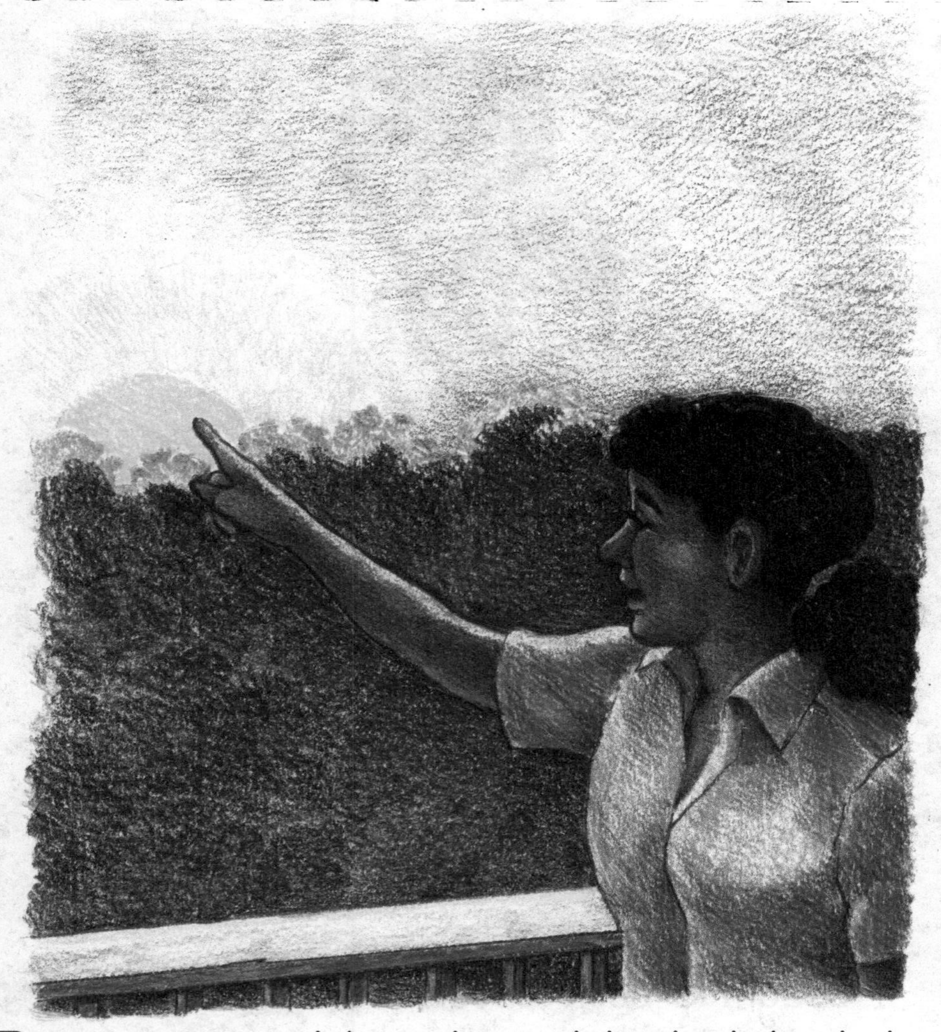

Dawn is a good time to spot birds. My dad taught me that dawn is when birds wake up.

I paused and looked at the hood of my auto.

Soon it was time to go. I had not spotted a bunting. I was disappointed!

I enjoyed visiting the woods every day before dawn. I brought my bird book. I looked for a bunting.

I hid in the woods. I crawled in tall grass. I fought annoying bugs! But I didn't spot a bunting.

I saw a yellow finch and a blackbird. But I did not see a bunting.

Small birds made loud noises. They saw the hawk. They tried to avoid being caught.

In the fall, the buntings had to fly away. I had to spot a bunting before then!

It was the last day of August. I hid in deep grass. I thought birds could not see me. I spotted a hawk.

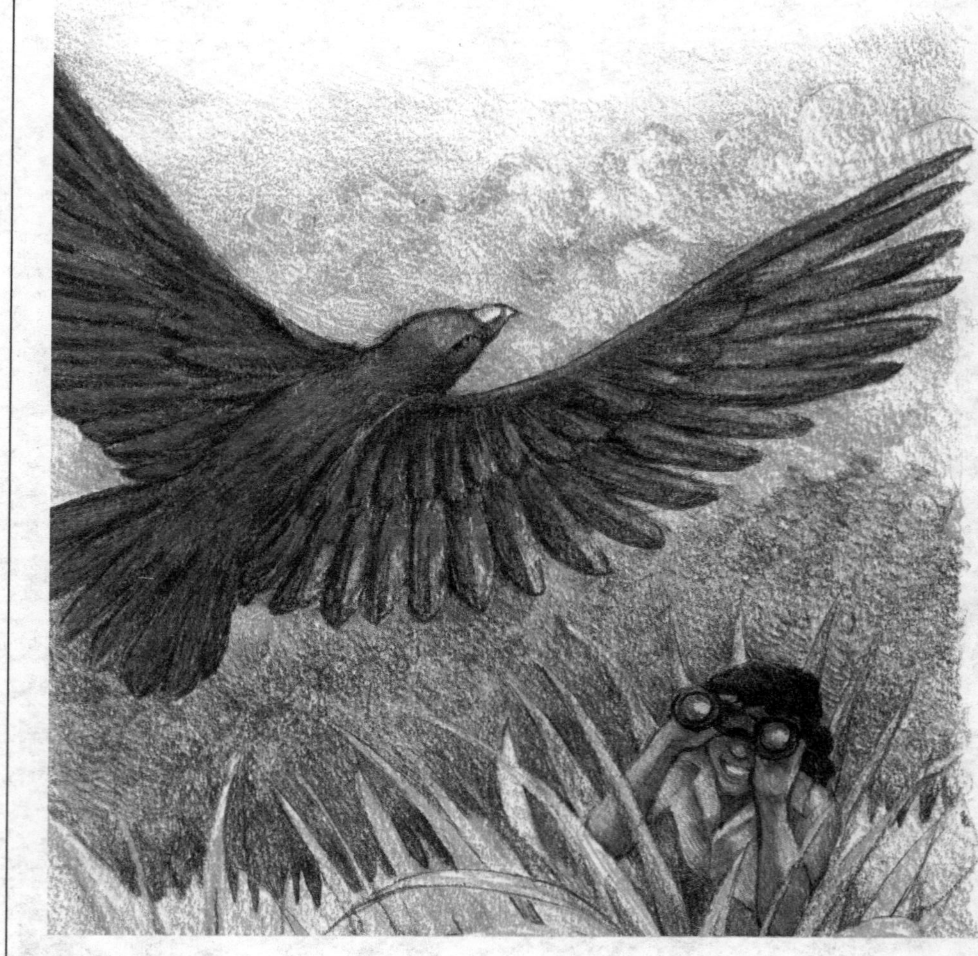

The hawk flew in a low circle. Was it because of me? No, it was looking for food.

Tom looked unhappy. "These things will get better," he whispered. Then he had to unplug more wires.

Mr. Paws Invents

by Aubrey Brown
illustrated by Marilyn Janovitz

Core Decodable 103

Mc Graw Hill Education

Bothell, WA • Chicago, IL • Columbus, OH • New York, NY

MHEonline.com

Mc Graw Hill Education

Send all inquiries to:
McGraw-Hill Education
8787 Orion Place
Columbus, OH 43240

"This is Tom. If he did not help me, I would be unable to make things," said Mr. Paws.

"This unzips and unpacks a bag," said Mr. Paws.

"It rips the bag. It rips shirts and pants!" whispered Tom.

"I invented this. It unscrews caps. It makes caps easy to open," Mr. Paws said.

"I dislike saying it, but this will not go well," Tom whispered.

Just then, bottles fell all over! Tom unplugged a red wire.

"No! It unmakes your bed. It shreds your mattress. It unstuffs your pillows!" Tom whispered.

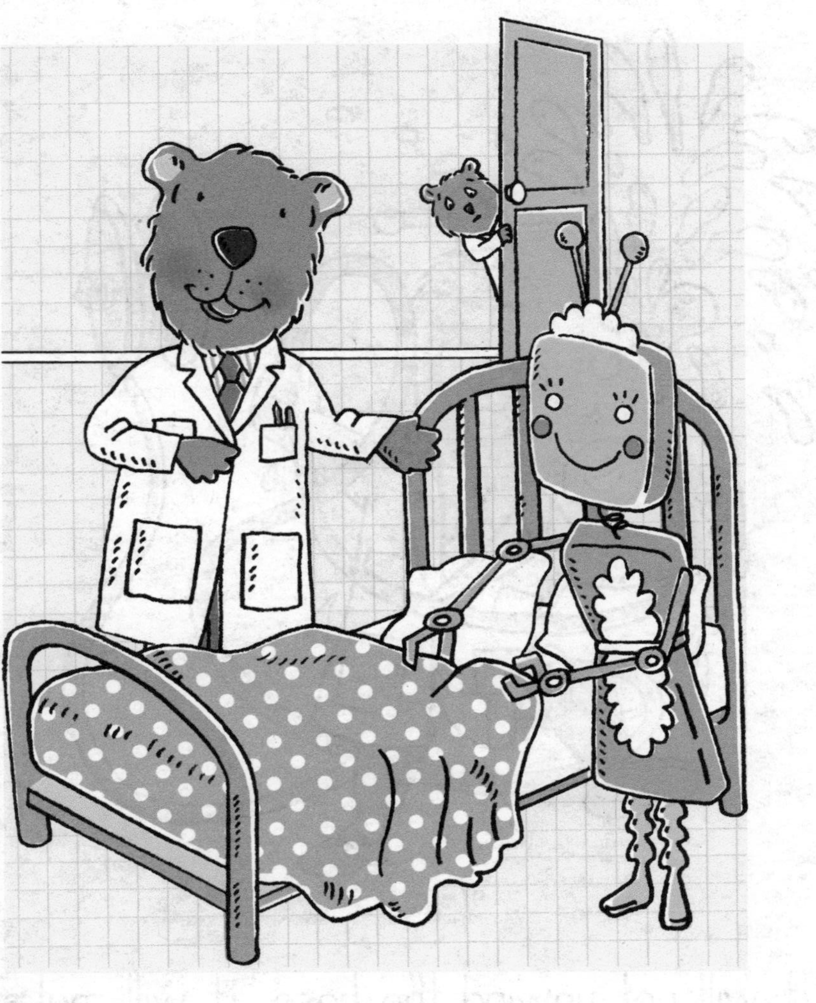

Mr. Paws went back in the lab. "Is your bed unmade? This can make it!" he said.

Mr. Paws said, "I invented this. It wraps and unwraps gifts."

"I disagree," Tom whispered. "It cannot wrap gifts and it cannot unwrap gifts! It can just smash gifts."

"It will not unwind the hose. It will make a knot!" whispered sad Tom.

He had to untie the hose.

Mr. Paws was in a yard. "This unwinds a hose. It unwinds a hose fast," he said.

Tom had to disconnect green wires. He had to untwist black wires.

Mr. Paws did not see the mess.

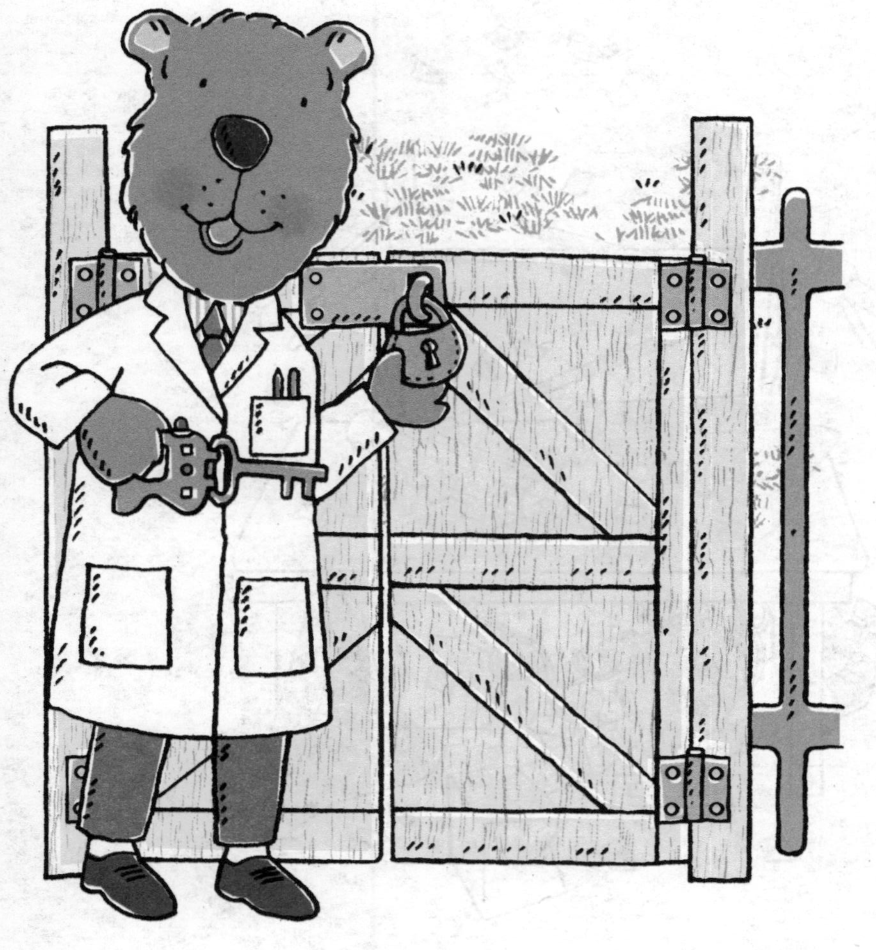

"This opens locks. It can unlock this gate," Mr. Paws explained.

"That is untrue! It jams locks!" whispered Tom. Tom had to yank the nails to get out.

Later Gram looked out. The boys had printed in the snow "Thanks Gram!" Gram said to herself, "Thanks Dad!"

Gram and the Kids

by Luke Anderson
illustrated by Luanne Marten

Core Decodable 104

Bothell, WA • Chicago, IL • Columbus, OH • New York, NY

MHEonline.com

McGraw Hill Education

Send all inquiries to:
McGraw-Hill Education
8787 Orion Place
Columbus, OH 43240

The boxes were wet now. The boys set them on the porch. Gram would recycle the boxes later.

Now the boys had a real snow fort!
The happy boys each hugged and rehugged Gram.

Gram stood inside the house. In the yard, the boys made a snow fort. Gram smiled.

The kids would try and retry to make snow walls. But the walls just looked like bumps.

The boys used and reused the boxes to make snow bricks. They stacked bricks on bricks.

Gram used the box to make a snow brick. Making a fort was not impossible for Gram!

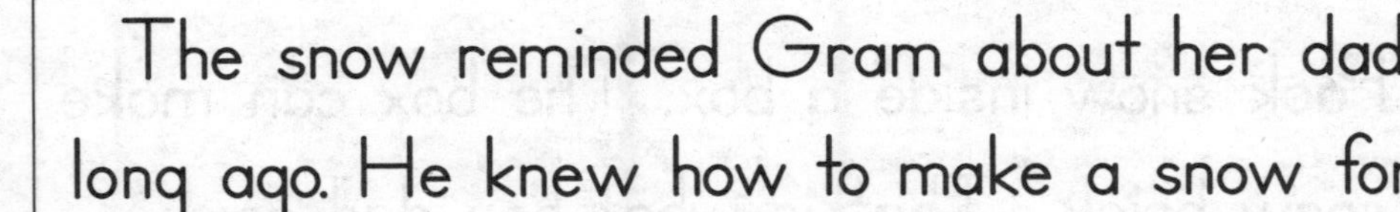

The snow reminded Gram about her dad long ago. He knew how to make a snow fort.

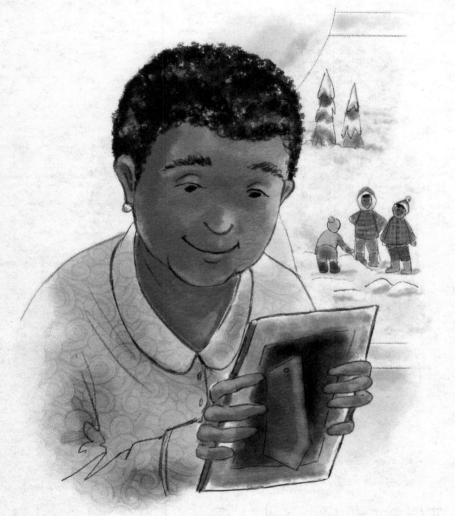

"Pack snow inside a box. The box can make a snow brick." That is what her dad said.

Could Gram make a fort? That seemed impossible! But Gram grabbed a box and packed snow in it.

The boys were surprised to see Gram. "Let me help you remake that fort," she said.

Gram did not like the cold much these days. But she could not stay inside. She wanted to help the boys!

Gram visited the basement to get empty boxes. They had held boots, books, and more stuff. Gram could reuse them.

Gram dressed in a heavy coat, mittens, and hat. "Thin clothes are improper for cold," her dad always said.

Jackie and Max walked around the rooftop garden. Plants filled the space.

"Wow! This is one big garden!" Jackie said.

Garden in the Sky

by Maria Johnson
illustrated by Len Ebert

Core Decodable 105

Bothell, WA • Chicago, IL • Columbus, OH • New York, NY

MHEonline.com

Mc Graw Hill Education

Send all inquiries to:
McGraw-Hill Education
8787 Orion Place
Columbus, OH 43240

The three walked out on the skyscraper roof. Jackie was shocked. All she could see was sky and plants.

Max's dad set stuff on his desk. "Time to go up," he said.

Soon the three were back on the elevator. They were going up.

Max and Jackie liked gardens.

"My dad's job is in a skyscraper," said Max. "It has a big garden."

"A garden in a skyscraper?" Jackie asked. "How can that be?"

"I will ask my dad to take us," said Max.

"This is a nice garden!" said Jackie.

"This is not it yet," said Max. "Just wait!"

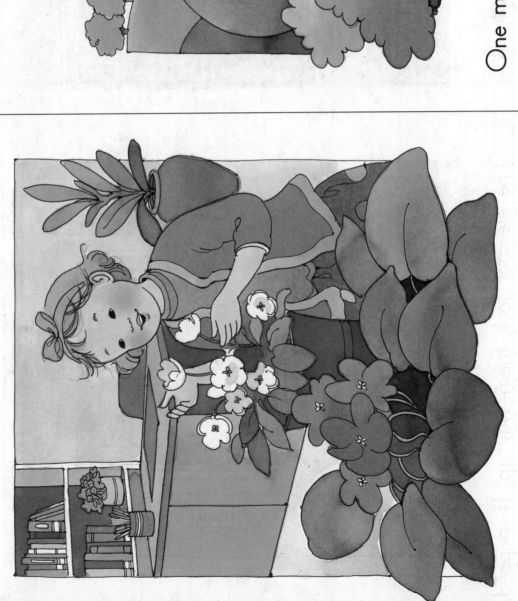

All around were plants and flowers. Jackie thought one flower was wax. But it was real.

One morning, Max's dad did take the kids. They rode the train. The train raced down the tracks.

Dad, Max, and Jackie were downtown fast. They walked to a tall skyscraper. It seemed to be made of dark glass.

The elevator took them way up. It stopped, and they walked out.

"My desk is back there," said Max's dad.

"That is not the garden," said Max.
Jackie thought it looked like one.
The three stepped on the elevator.

"This is the place," said Max.
Jackie looked way up. "Wow!" she said.

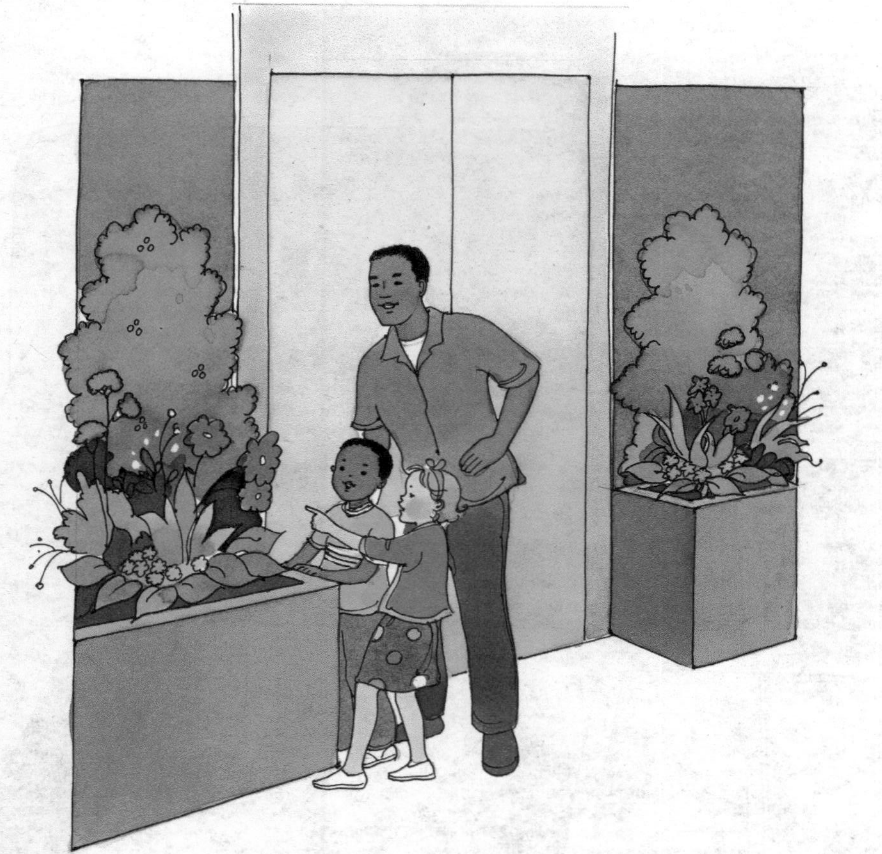

On the sidewalk, there were big planters.
They were filled with plants.
"Is this the garden?" asked Jackie.
"No way," said Max.

The three walked inside. A man with a badge said, "Good day."
By the man's desk were plants.

"That's right," said Ranger Liz. "So what do you say now, Rick?"

"Please do not pick the flowers," smiled Rick.

Picking Flowers

by Charles Broderick
illustrated by Dennis Hockerman

Core Decodable 106

Bothell, WA • Chicago, IL • Columbus, OH • New York, NY

MHEonline.com

McGraw-Hill Education

Send all inquiries to:
McGraw-Hill Education
8787 Orion Place
Columbus, OH 43240

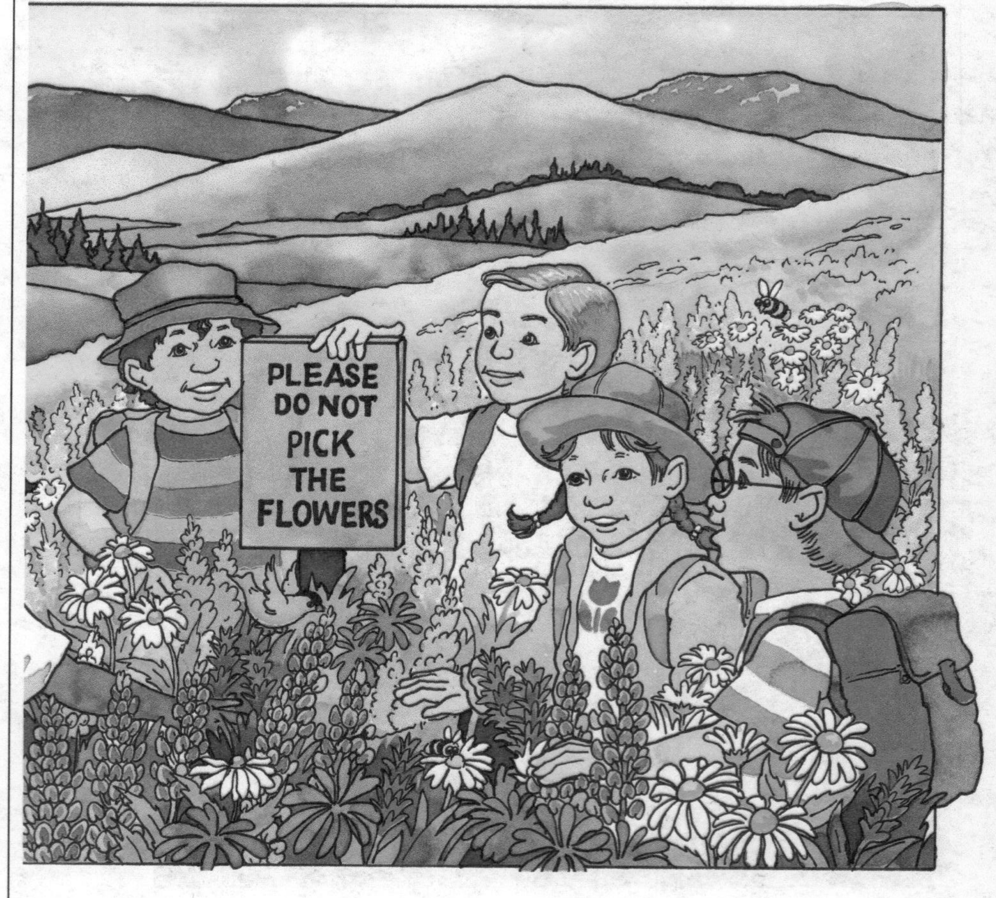

Rick was thinking. "There would be no flowers left," he said. "And that would be bad for the bees and birds."

"That's a lot of flowers," said Liz. "And hundreds of kids hike here each week. What if all those kids picked flowers?"

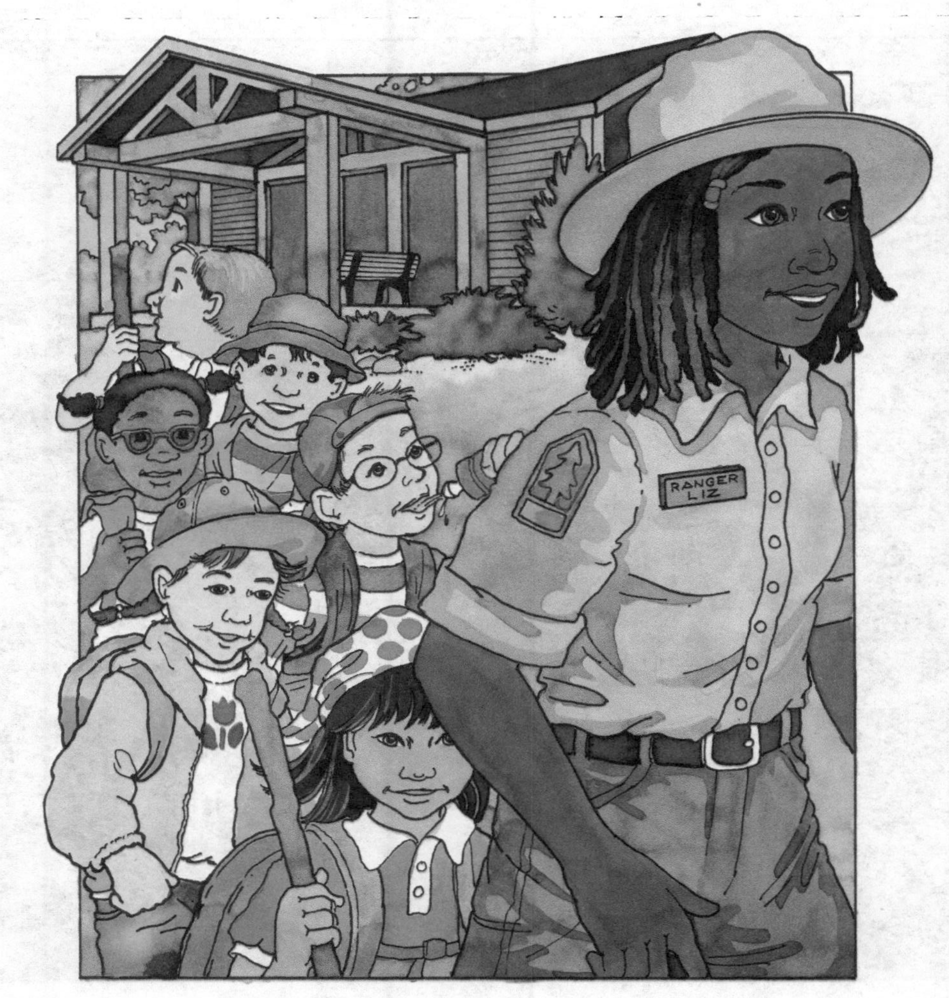

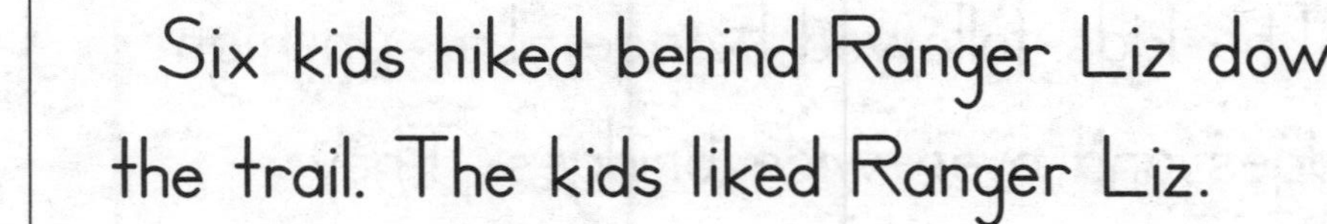

Six kids hiked behind Ranger Liz down the trail. The kids liked Ranger Liz.

The kids followed Ranger Liz up high ridges and over wide bridges. They followed her into a field of flowers.

"That's right," said Rick.

"What about your five pals?" asked Liz. "Would they like a mix, too?"

"Yes!" shouted the kids.

"Well," said Ranger Liz. "Your mom might like a mix of flowers. You might pick six or seven."

The kids really liked the flowers. Some flowers reached the trail's edge. Some looked like bright spikes.

"I wish I could take some flowers home," said Rick. "They would be nice for my mom."

"Read this," said Mike.

Rick was still thinking about his mom.

"But why can't we pick flowers?" he asked.

Ranger Liz smiled.

"See the bees and the birds," said Ranger Liz. "They need the flowers. And the flowers need them."

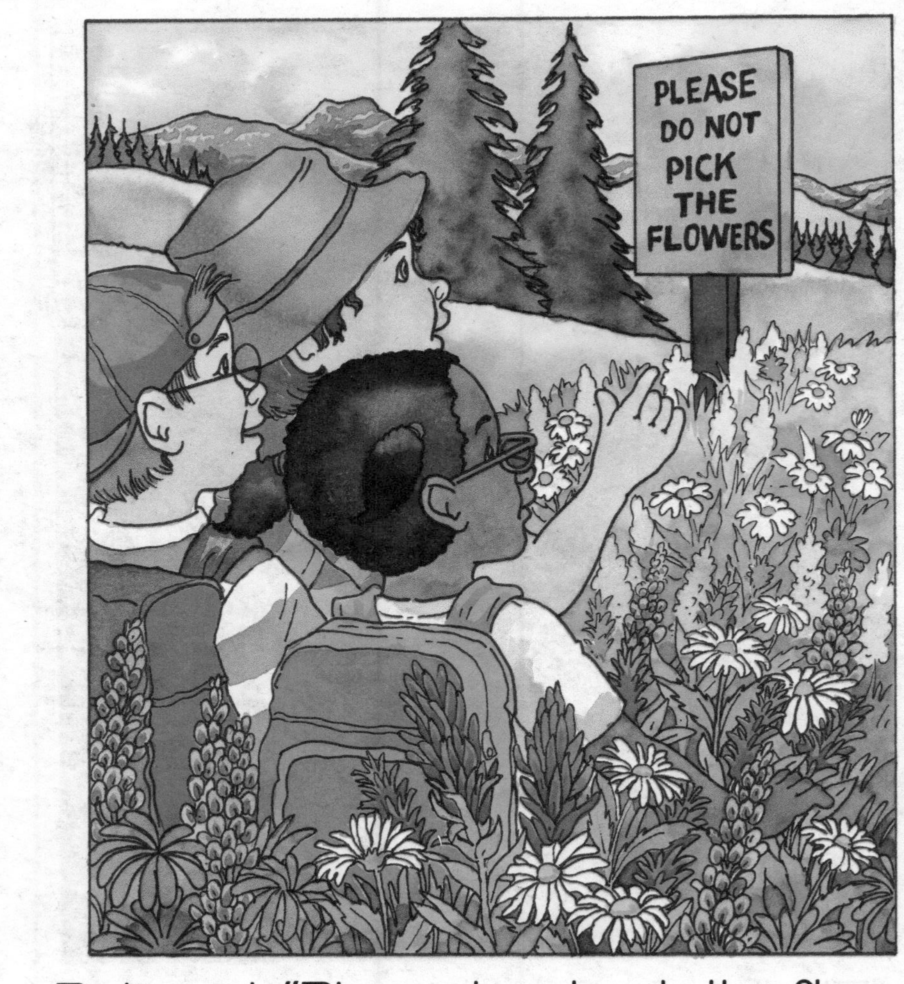

Rick read, "Please do not pick the flowers." Rick looked around the field. It was filled with flowers.

"There are miles of flowers," said Rick. "Why can't we pick some?"

A yellow and black bee buzzed by.

The bee sniffed at a flower. Rick and the kids jumped back. Then Rick saw a black and yellow finch. The bird sniffed at a flower, too.

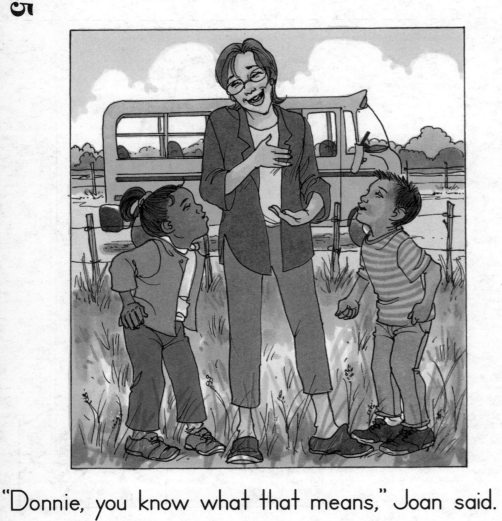

"Donnie, you know what that means," Joan said.

"Yes," smiled Donnie. "Moo!"

"Moo!" joined in Joan.

A Farm Visit

by William Overturf
illustrated by Meredith Johnson

Core Decodable 107

Bothell, WA • Chicago, IL • Columbus, OH • New York, NY

MHEonline.com

McGraw Hill Education

Send all inquiries to:
McGraw-Hill Education
8787 Orion Place
Columbus, OH 43240

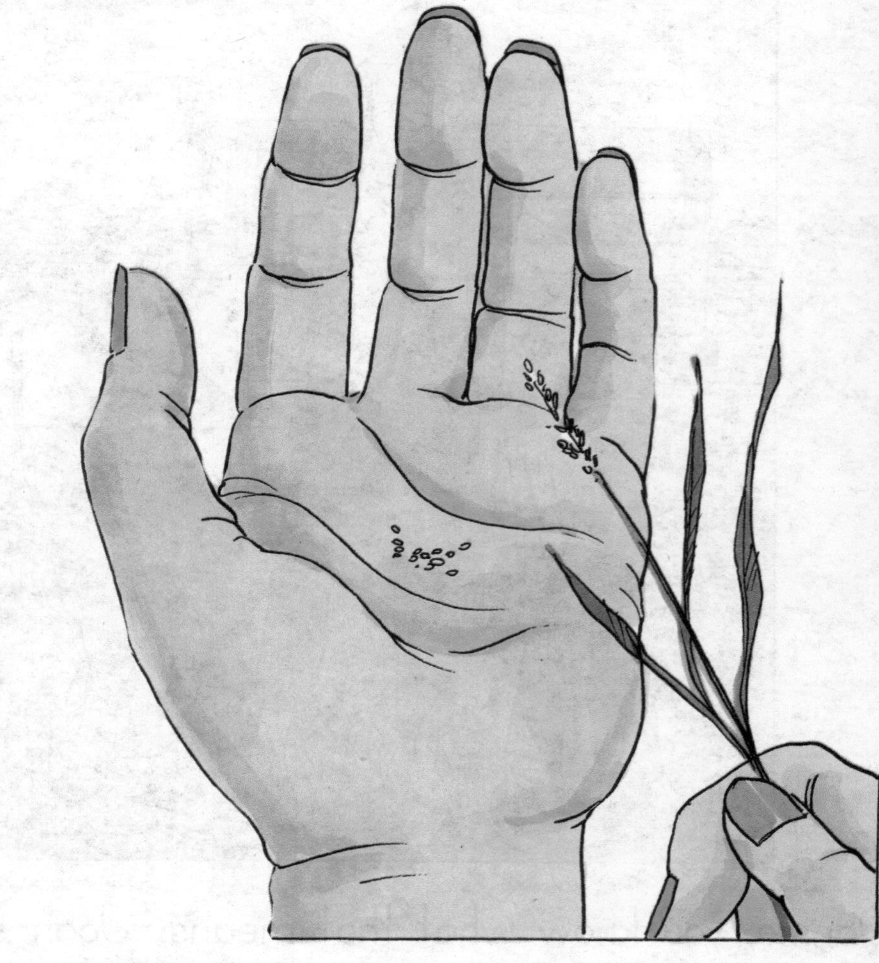

"Rice is a grass," said Miss Dock. "Seeds from it make food. And seeds from oat grass make food, too."

"Look," said Miss Dock. "This blade of grass has little seeds on top."

Miss Dock dropped little seeds in her hand.

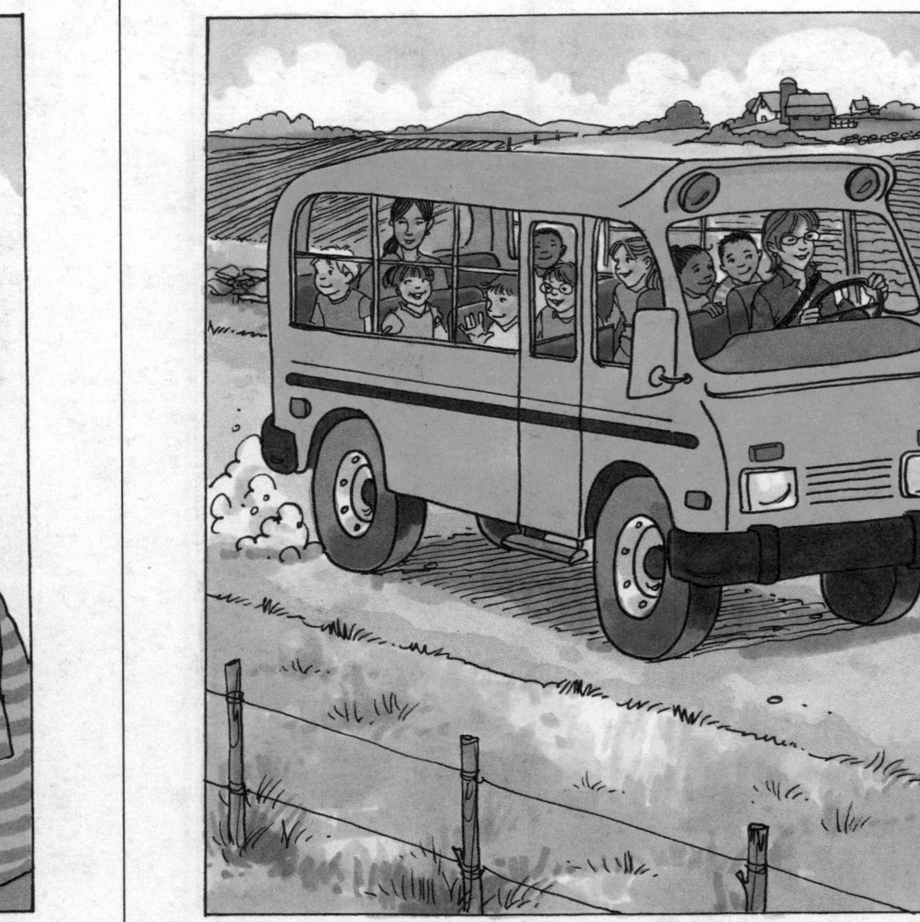

Miss Dock drove the bus to a farm. The class looked out the windows. They saw meadows, barns, and silos.

Some of the meadows had wire fences.
Some had low stone walls.
"Those stone walls have big rocks," said Joan.

Miss Dock and the kids got out of the bus. She picked a piece of very tall grass from the lawn.

Miss Dock parked the bus at the farmer's house. She looked at the farmer's lawn.

"I will show you," said Miss Dock.

The kids were from the city. Some had never seen a farm.

"Is that an ox?" asked Donnie.

Miss Dock smiled. "Nope, it looks a bit like an ox. But it is just a big cow."

"Ick! It is eating grass," said Joan.

"Rice is grass?" asked Joan.

"Oatmeal is not green," said Donnie. "How can oats be grass?"

The bus was going slowly down the road. The road had big holes. Miss Dock had to dodge them.

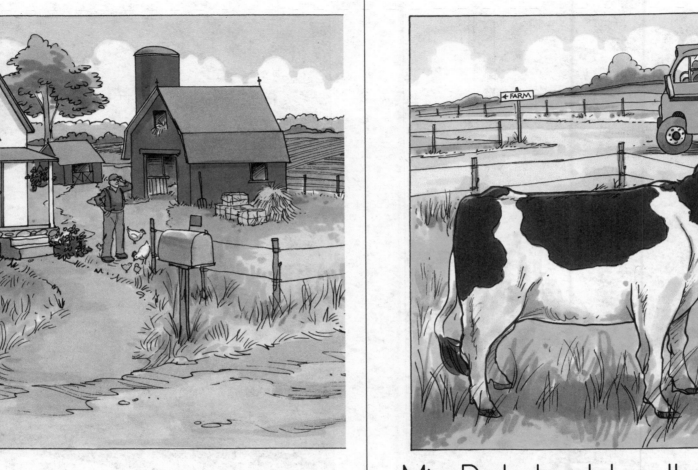

Miss Dock slowed down the bus. "We eat grass, too," she said.

"No way!" said Joan.

The cow was mooing now.

Miss Dock drove the bus over a bumpy road.

"What did you eat for breakfast?" Miss Dock asked.

"A little box of Rice Puffs," Joan said.

"A bowl of oatmeal," said Donnie.

"You both had grass, then," said Miss Dock.

Mr. Plant Expert looked at the clock. "Thanks kids! Thanks adults! I must run to pluck some weeds. See you next time!"

Mr. Plant Expert

by Sidney Allen
illustrated by Dominic Catalano

Core Decodable 108

Bothell, WA • Chicago, IL • Columbus, OH • New York, NY

MHEonline.com

McGraw Hill Education

Send all inquiries to:
McGraw-Hill Education
8787 Orion Place
Columbus, OH 43240

"Do plants like music? What tunes do they like?" asked a girl.

"Plant experts like music," said Mr. Expert. "I like rock tunes."

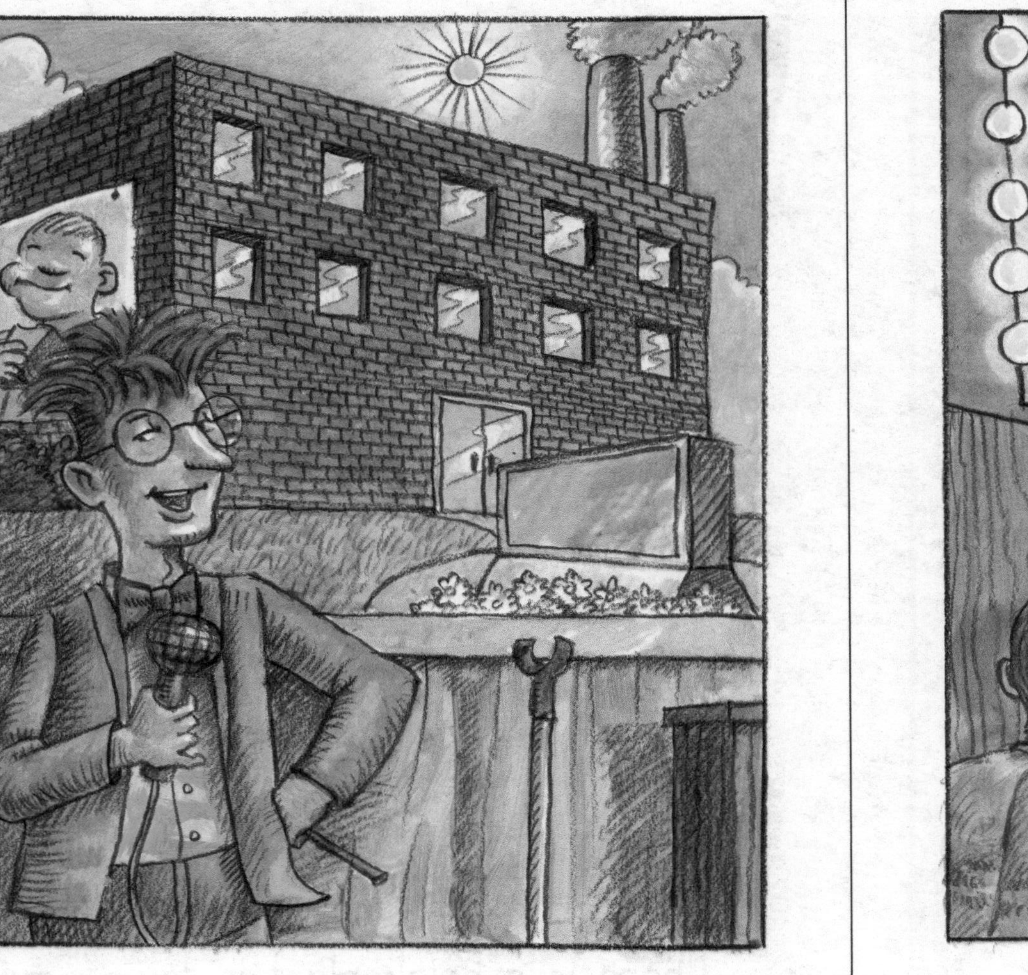

"Plant can mean factory," said Mr. Expert. "A factory makes things. A brick plant makes bricks."

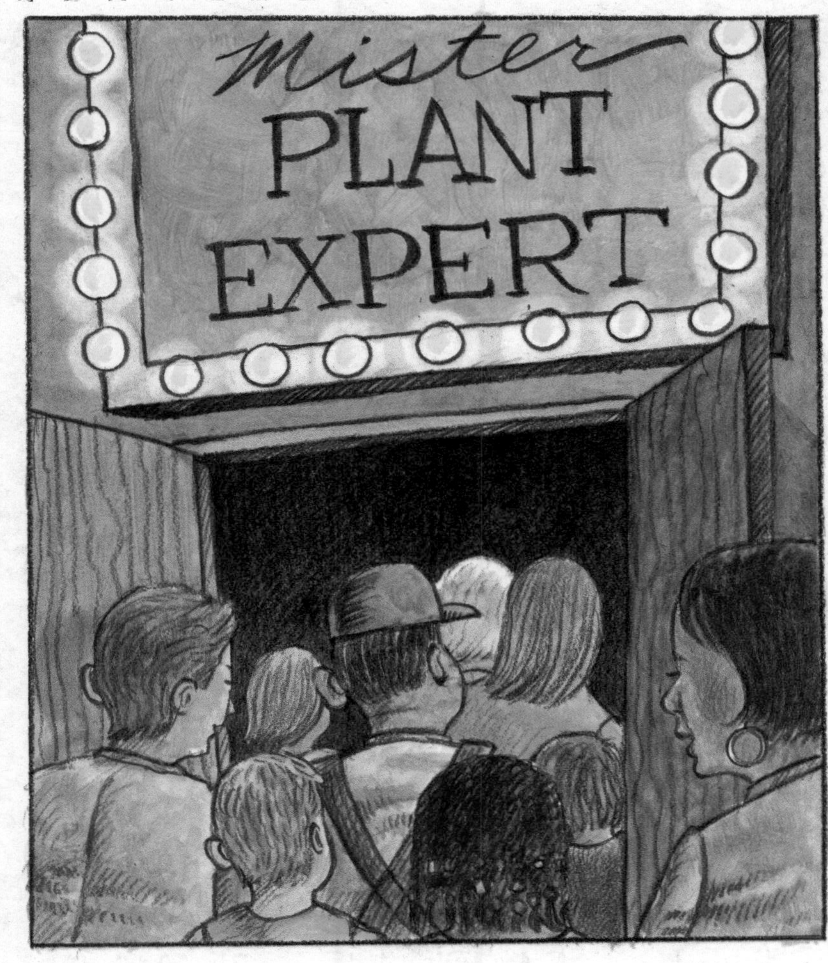

Kids and adults filled the hall. They came to see Mr. Plant Expert. They came to have fun.

"Hi! I am Mr. Plant Expert. Ask me about plants and gardens. Maybe you can stump me!"

"There is a brick plant in town," said a boy. "Can bricks grow on plants?"

"No," said Mr. Expert.

"I am a good gardener," explained Mr. Expert. "That is what a green thumb means. But my thumbs are not really green."

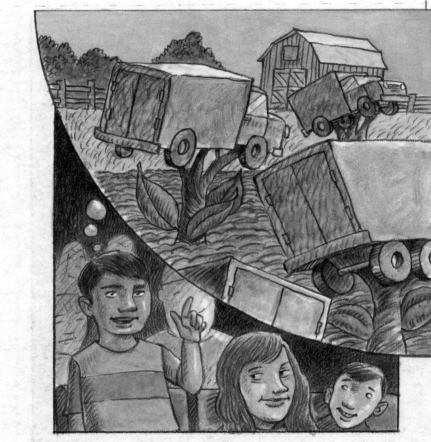

"Mr. Expert," said a pupil. "I heard about a truck farm. Do huge trucks grow there? Are buses and cars grown there, too?"

"No," smiled Mr. Expert. "Veggies grow on truck farms. The veggies are cucumbers, beans, and so on."

"My mom said you have a green thumb. Can I see it?" asked a cute kid.

Mr. Expert chuckled.

"Bugs eat plants," said a man. "But do plants eat bugs?"

"A few do," said Mr. Expert. "They are good to take to picnics."

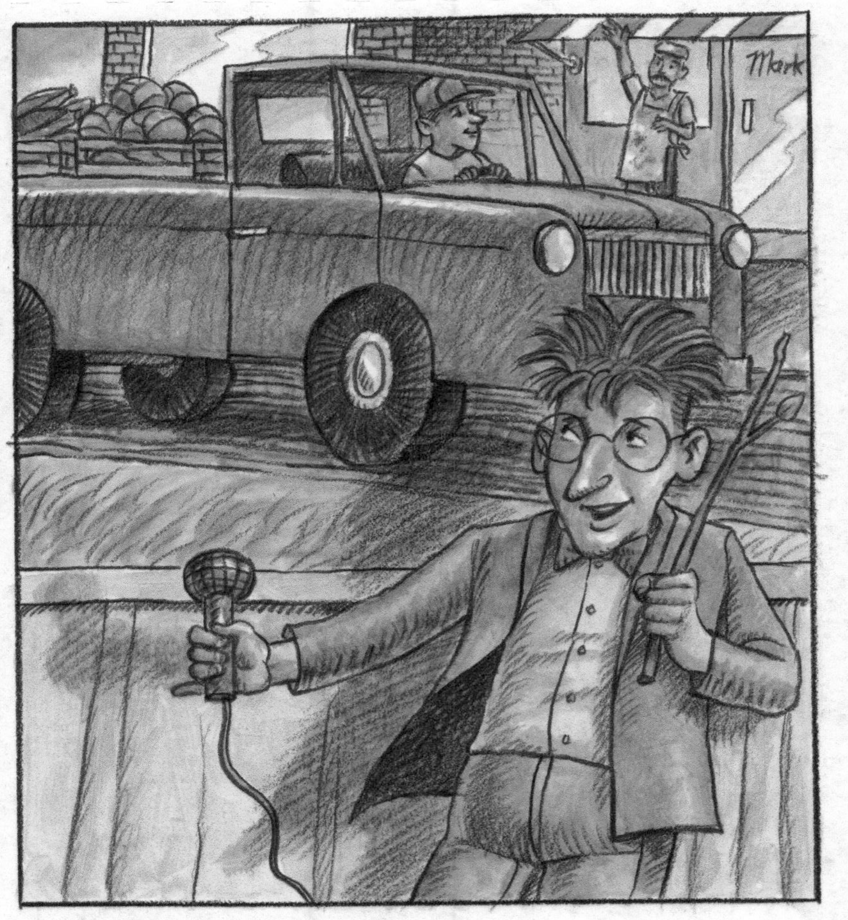

"Farmers pack veggies in boxes. Trucks take the veggies to stores. That is why the farms are called truck farms."

"Is this true?" asked a boy. "Do plants get fuel from the sun? How can a hose reach that far?"

"Plants do get fuel from the sun," explained Mr. Expert. "But plants do not use hoses. Sunshine provides plants with fuel."

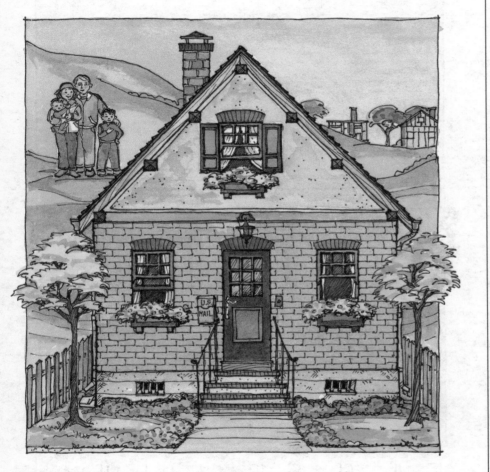

The family of four stood on the grassy hill. They looked at the new house below.

"We are so lucky," Dean said.

A Family House

by Ethan Cruz
illustrated by Renate Lohmann

Core Decodable 109

Bothell, WA • Chicago, IL • Columbus, OH • New York, NY

MHEonline.com

Mc Graw Hill Education

Send all inquiries to:
McGraw-Hill Education
8787 Orion Place
Columbus, OH 43240

Finally, after weeks and weeks, the house was ready. A big van brought beds, dressers, desks, and tables.

Four trees were planted. Carpenters put a deck on the back of the house.

"We will eat there at times," said Mom.

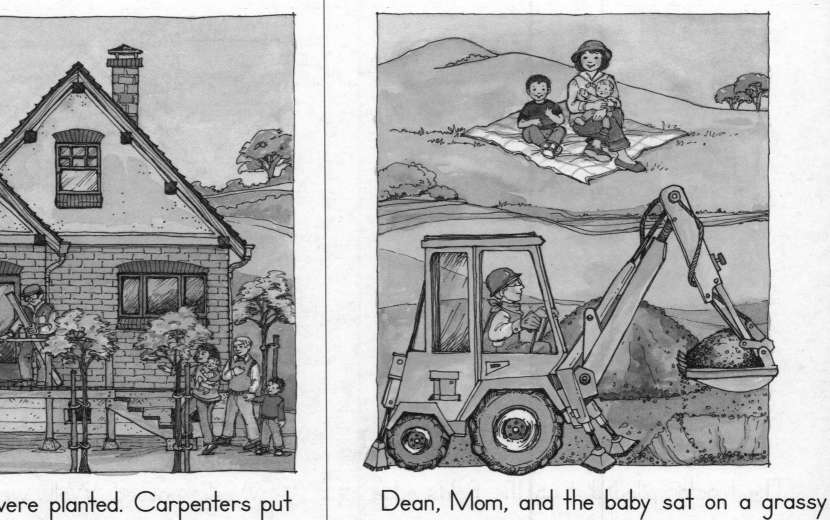

Dean, Mom, and the baby sat on a grassy hill. A tractor dug below. The tractor dug a deep hole.

The tractor piled dirt on the field's edge. "That hole will be the basement," explained Mom. "And trucks will haul that dirt away."

Weeks passed. Walls were plastered. Lights and switches were added. Painters came. Soon the house was almost ready.

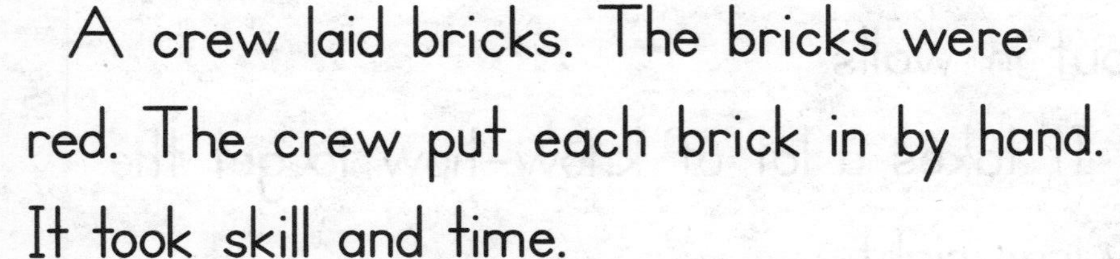

A crew laid bricks. The bricks were red. The crew put each brick in by hand. It took skill and time.

Dean was happy. This hole was the start of a new house. It was his family's new house! He felt lucky.

A week later, Dean and Mom came back. The hole now had cement walls. On top, it had four steel beams.

Electric wires were added. Wires were put in walls.

It takes a lot of know-how to get the wires right.

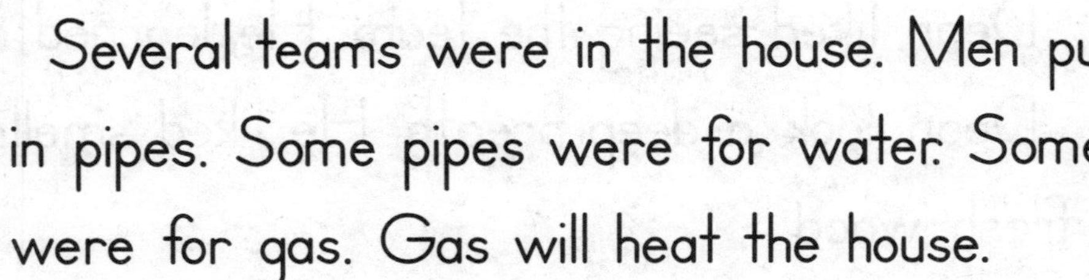

Several teams were in the house. Men put in pipes. Some pipes were for water. Some were for gas. Gas will heat the house.

"Steel beams will hold up the house," said Mom. Three weeks later, Dean was back. A team of four carpenters hammered.

The frame went up quickly. Dad also came to check the house.

Dad pointed. "You will sleep in a bedroom there."

Dean liked seeing the team. He learned a lot.

Dean took a deep breath. He liked smelling fresh wood.

Josh looked out the window.

"I see the truth," he thought. "Ruth's nephew has just one house. It has wheels!"

Houses

by Maria Johnson
illustrated by Doug Roy

Core Decodable 110

McGraw Hill Education

Bothell, WA • Chicago, IL • Columbus, OH • New York, NY

MHEonline.com

Mc Graw Hill Education

Send all inquiries to:
McGraw-Hill Education
8787 Orion Place
Columbus, OH 43240

In September, Josh's phone rang. "Josh, this is Ruth," said a voice. "I am calling from my nephew's house in the street."

"That is his fifth house!" thought Josh. "Ruth's nephew must be very, very rich."

But Josh still did not say that.

Sunshine filled the yard. Josh rested on his shady porch. It was hot for the third week in May.

At the next house, Ruth checked her mail. "My nephew sent a postcard," she called. "He is in his house on the beach."

In August, Josh brushed his dog's fur. "My nephew sent a photo," said Ruth. "He is in his house in the far north."

Josh was shocked. "Four houses!" he thought.
"How can Ruth's nephew own four houses?"
But Josh did not say that.

"His house is on the beach!" Josh thought.
"I wish I had a house on the beach."
But he did not say that.

In early June, Josh painted a bench.

"My nephew wrote me," Ruth said. "He is in his house at the ranch."

Later, Ruth said, "I got a call from my nephew. He is in his house in the woods. He is searching for birds."

It was later in the summer. Josh was making lunch for a bunch of pals. He heard a phone ring in Ruth's house.

"Wow," thought Josh. "Ruth's nephew has two houses! How did he pay for both?"

But he did not say that.

In late June, Josh cleaned his car.

"I heard from my nephew," Ruth said. "He is in his house at the river."

Now Josh thought, "Ruth's nephew must be rich. He has three houses."

But Josh did not say that.

Later in the summer, Dad placed tin over the rolled-up awning. Birds cannot make a nest there. We can use the awning. Dad learned!

A Summer Home

by Tom Sato
illustrated by Robin Kerr

Core Decodable 111

Bothell, WA • Chicago, IL • Columbus, OH • New York, NY

MHEonline.com

McGraw-Hill Education

Send all inquiries to:
McGraw-Hill Education
8787 Orion Place
Columbus, OH 43240

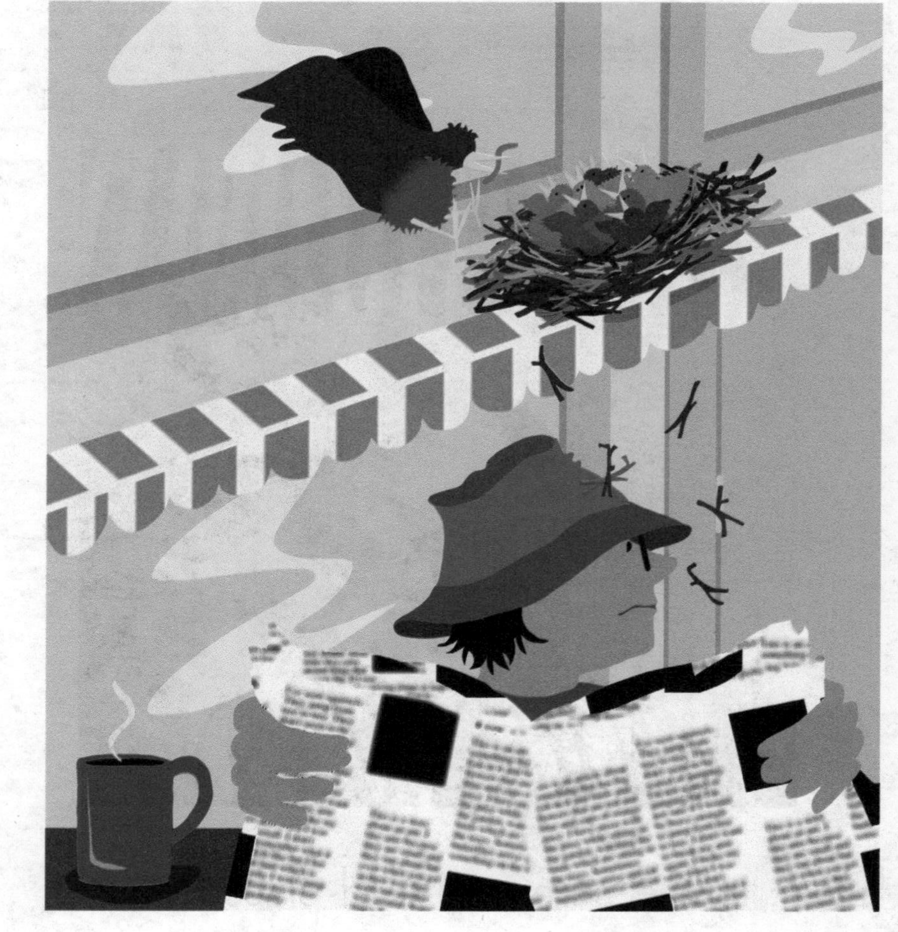

All summer, Dad did not start the motor.
And he did not open the awning.
New birds were born and grew.

I was concerned. Would Dad brush the nest away? He did not.

"Now this nest is a home," he said.

Last summer, Dad was thrilled. He had a large new awning! It was green and white. It could shade the backyard porch.

It was not hard to open the awning. Dad just hit a button. A little motor turned on, and the awning rolled out.

On Thursday, we came back. On the porch, Dad heard a bird. He grabbed his ladder.

"A nest with eggs!" he whispered.

"See," said Dad. "The bird is smart. It searched for a better place."

The next Sunday we visited a farm.

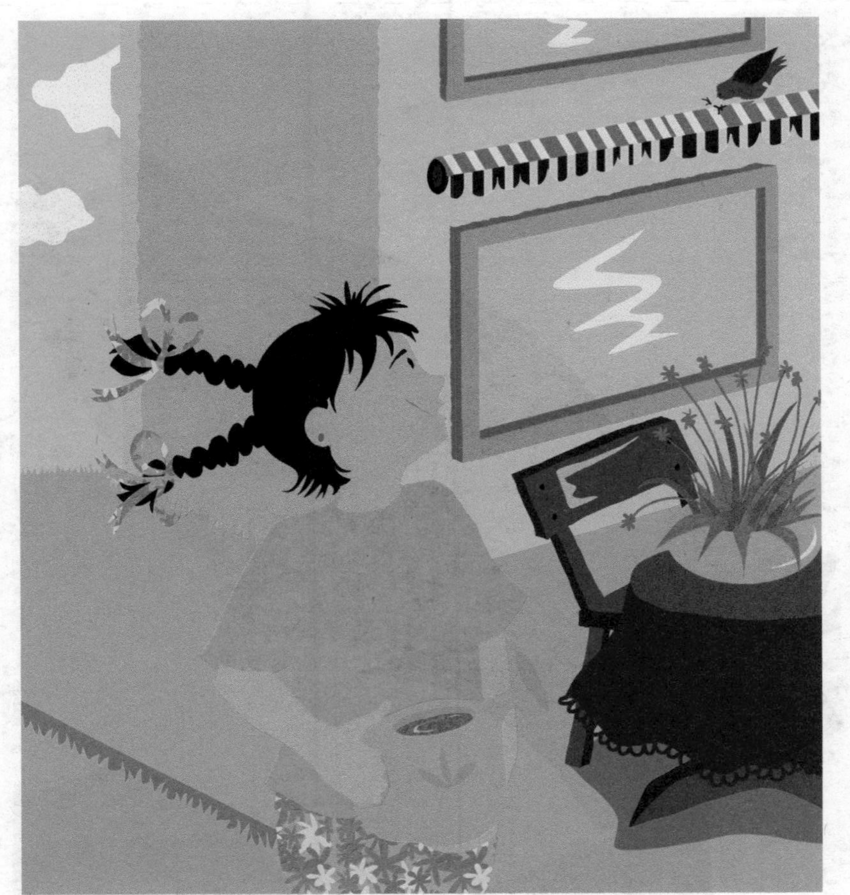

Early one day, I was on the porch. The awning was rolled up. I heard a bird. I looked up.

A bird was perched on the rolled-up awning. It had started to make a nest there. I called Dad.

Each day, Dad brushed the twigs away. After the third day, the bird stopped. It must have made a nest far away.

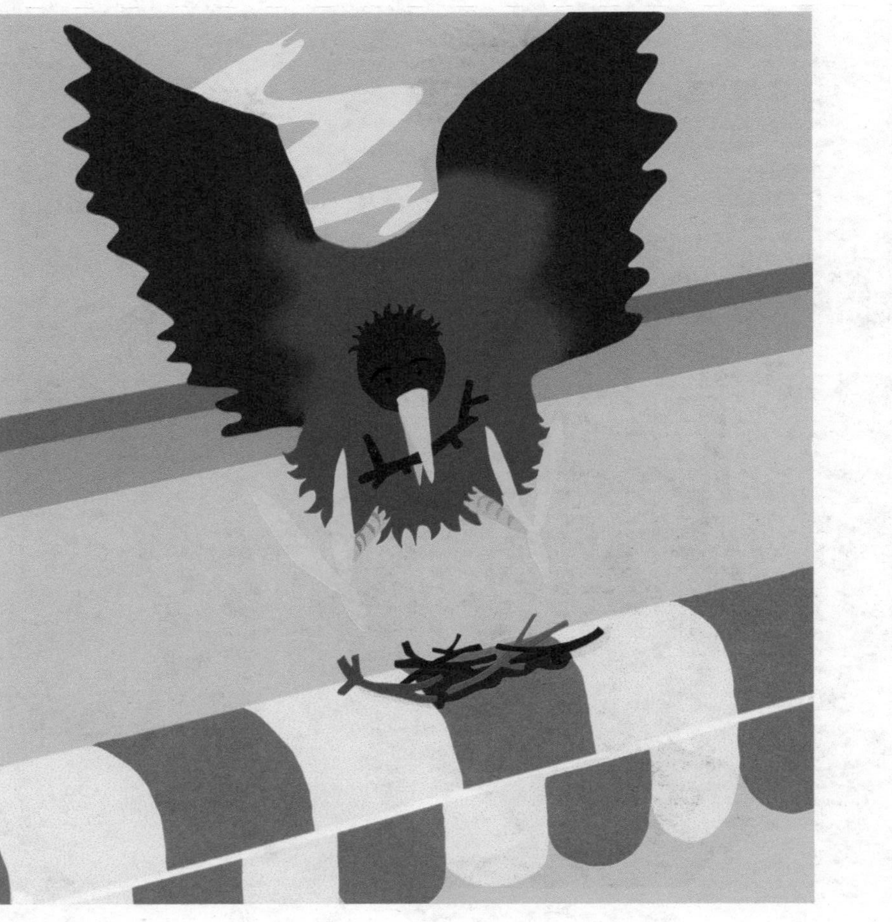

At first, the bird did not learn. Each day it perched on the awning. Each day, it started to make a nest.

The bird flew away. In a hurry, Dad grabbed a short ladder. He climbed up it. He looked at the nest.

"So far, this is just twigs," Dad said. He brushed them away.

"The bird will learn not to make a nest here."

I was surprised. Dad could tell.

"Do not be concerned," he said. "This will not hurt the bird. It will learn."

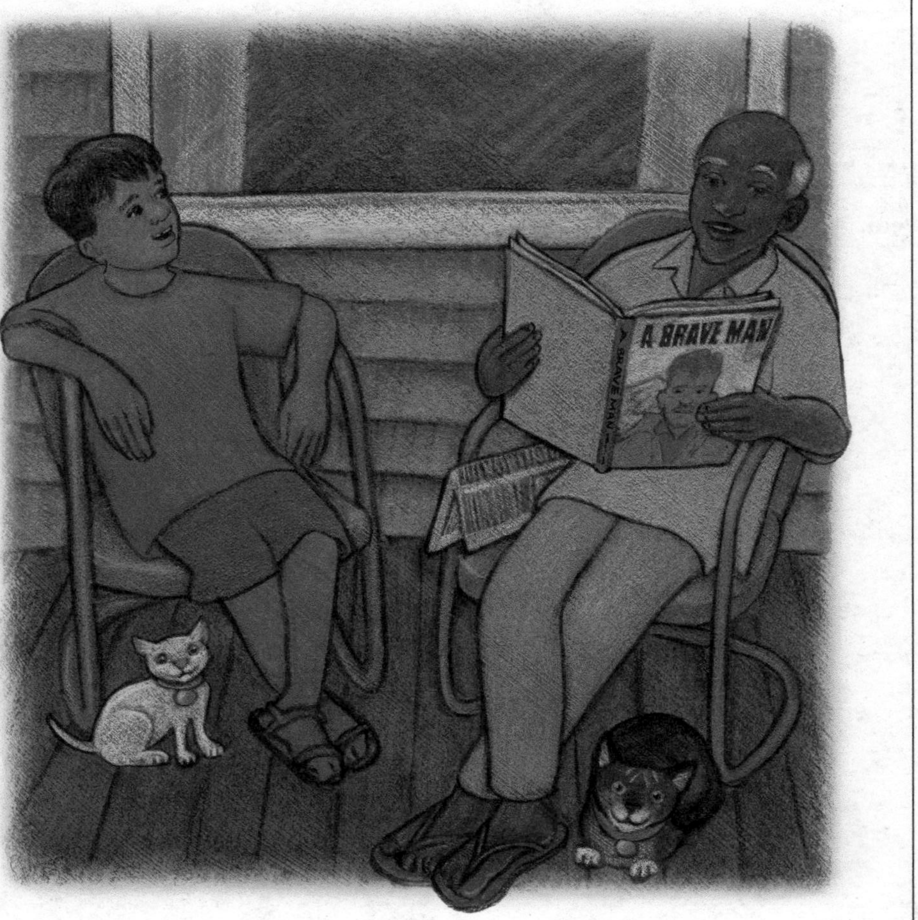

Mr. Bloom saw Tony's book. "I like that brave climber," he said.

He and Tony talked and talked. Brave Tony made a good pal.

Brave Tony

by Dennis Fertig
illustrated by Siri Weber Feeney

Core Decodable 112

McGraw Hill Education

Bothell, WA • Chicago, IL • Columbus, OH • New York, NY

MHEonline.com

McGraw Hill Education

Send all inquiries to:
McGraw-Hill Education
8787 Orion Place
Columbus, OH 43240

Tony told him in a nice way. Mr. Bloom smiled and said, "Tony, you are right. I will turn down that light."

"Hi, Tony," said Mr. Bloom.

"Hi, Mr. Bloom," said Tony. Then Tony followed his plan. He told Mr. Bloom about the light.

A Bright Light

On a hot night, Tony liked his window and blinds open. Then he could feel cool breezes. He could see the moon.

Lately, a bright light changed things. It filled Tony's room. He had to shut his blinds. The light came from the next house.

The next afternoon, Tony went to Mr. Bloom. Tony carried the book with him. It helped him act bravely.

Tony thought about how the brave man climbed the peak. That man made a good plan. Tony would, too.

The house was Mr. Bloom's. He was new on the block. He did not talk much. He just stood and looked at plants.

Now Tony was not thinking about Mr. Bloom. Tony was reading a good book. It was about a brave man.

A Good Plan

Tony knew what he had to do. He had to talk to Mr. Bloom soon. But Tony felt afraid.

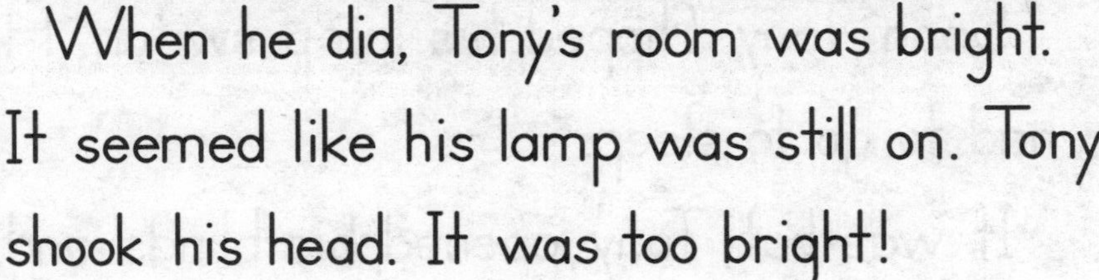

When he did, Tony's room was bright. It seemed like his lamp was still on. Tony shook his head. It was too bright!

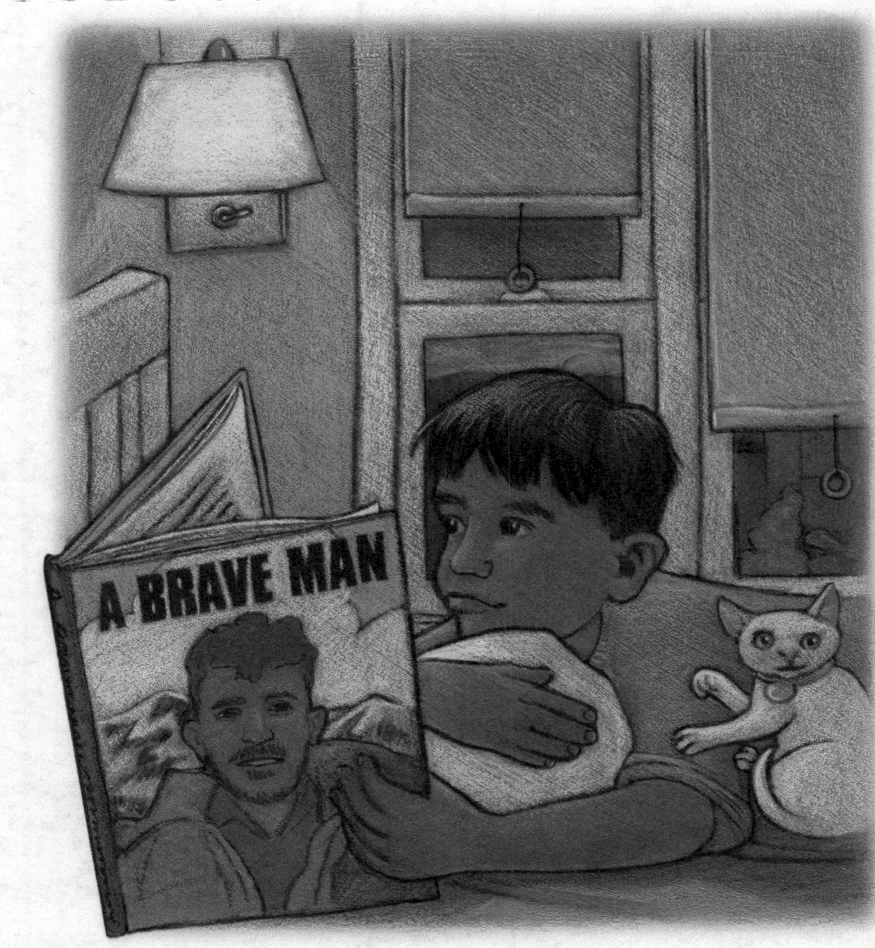

The man took a chance. He climbed the highest peak on Earth. The man was brave, but not foolish. He made good plans.

The book was true. The man was real. Tony liked true books. He liked them better than made-up books.

Soon Tony flipped his lamp switch. He had to go to sleep.

It was hot. Tony opened his blinds and window.

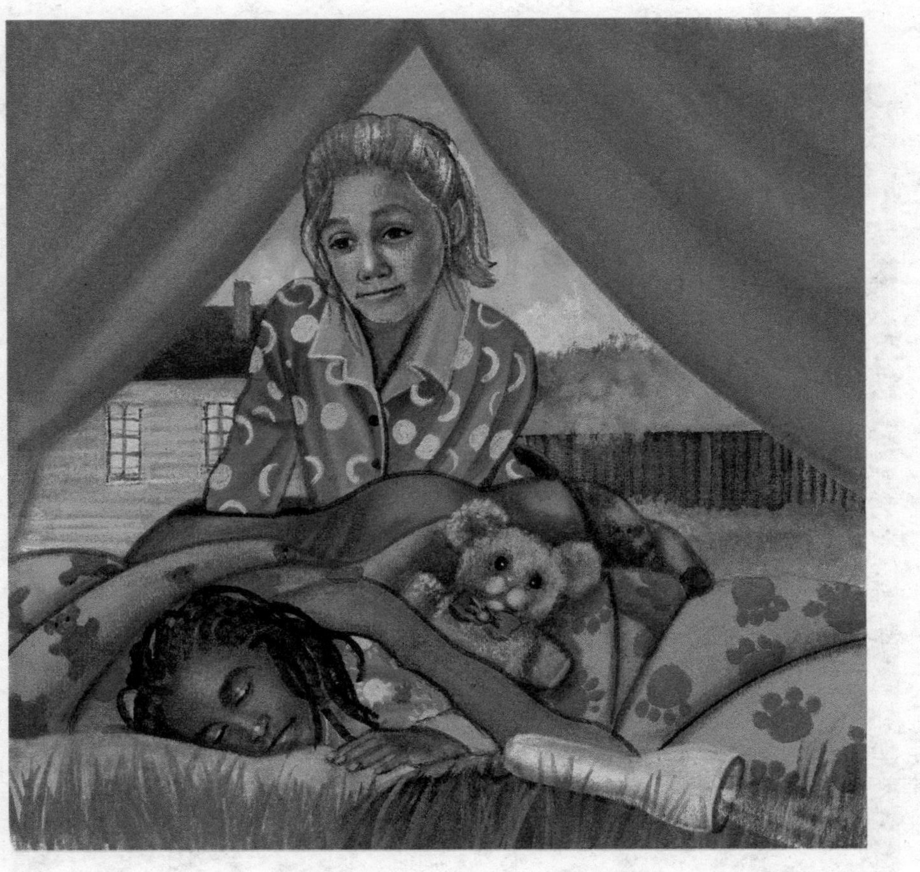

The sun woke Brook up. "I slept well," she said. Audrey did not say a thing. She was sound asleep at last.

Camping Out

by William Overturf
illustrated by Carol Heyer

Core Decodable 113

Bothell, WA • Chicago, IL • Columbus, OH • New York, NY

MHEonline.com

Mc Graw Hill Education

Send all inquiries to:
McGraw-Hill Education
8787 Orion Place
Columbus, OH 43240

Audrey was awake for a long, long time. She thought she heard a mouse. She thought she heard a shout.

And Brook just slept.

Audrey slid down in her sleeping bag. She felt so afraid. She did not even have the power to talk.

Plans for a Camp Out

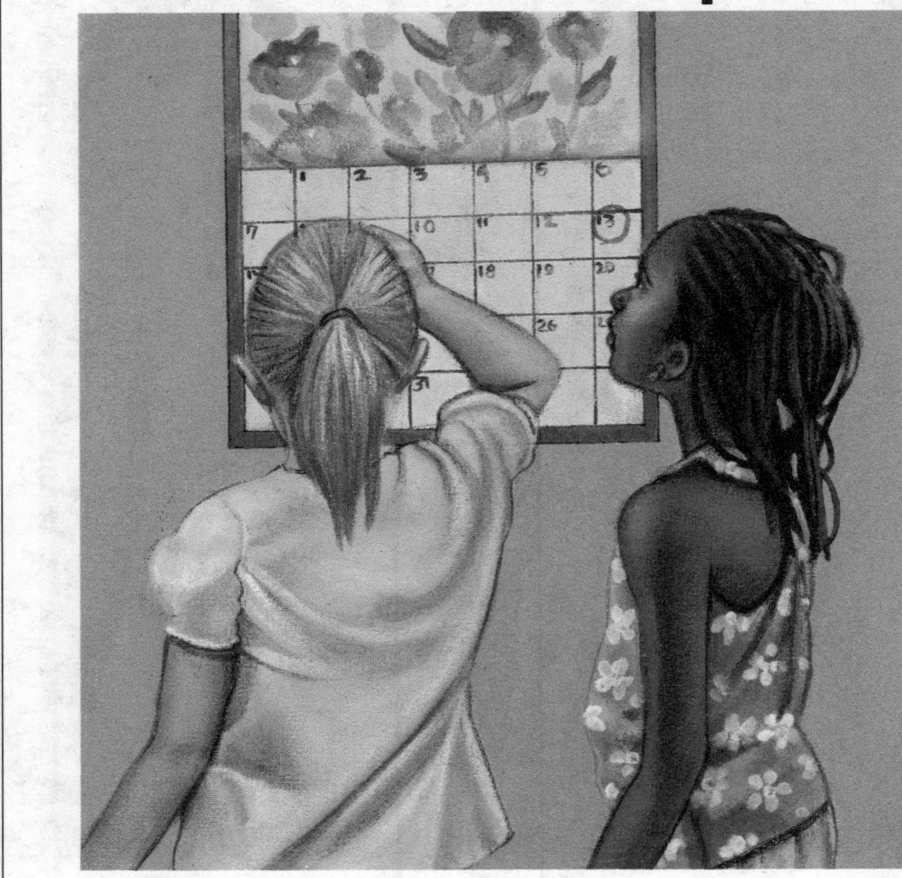

The girls waited all week. On Saturday, they would camp out. They would sleep on the ground in a tent.

"I hope I will not be afraid," said Brook. "I have never camped before."

"We will be right in town," said Audrey.

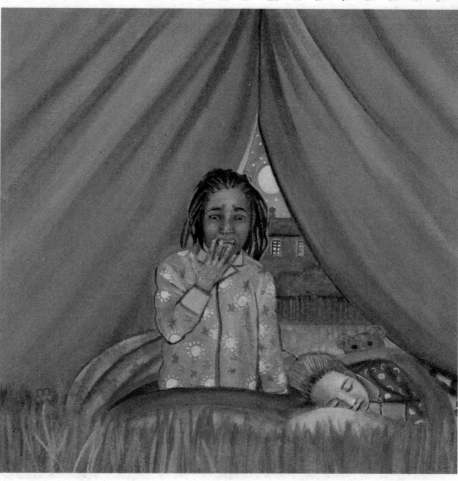

Then Audrey heard a loud howl! She jumped. Her hand felt the cold, moist soil. There might be bugs in the ground!

Audrey felt very afraid. What could she do? Call her mom? Run to the house?

"I must stay," she frowned.

"And we will be next to my house. My mom and dad will be around," Audrey added. "You will enjoy camping out."

At last, it was Saturday night. Audrey's dad made dinner. He grilled corn in foil. He also made sweet and sour chicken.

Audrey heard a loud sound. Was it a growl? There was more noise. Was an animal prowling around?

Brook just slept.

Afraid in the Tent

Brook quickly fell asleep. Audrey did not. She felt afraid!

"Being afraid is stupid," she thought. "I am right by my house."

At nine, there were no clouds in the dark sky. The girls saw the round moon and a thousand stars.

Audrey's mom and dad said good night.

The girls crawled in the tent.

"Are you afraid, Brook?" asked Audrey.

Brook thought about it.

She was surprised. She did not feel afraid.

"Wow," said Brook. "I feel fine now."

Andy was an artist. His glass made rainbows dance in rooms. It also made him brave.

Andy Lee

by Jennifer Jacobson
illustrated by Jon Agee

Core Decodable 114

Bothell, WA • Chicago, IL • Columbus, OH • New York, NY

MHEonline.com

Mc Graw Hill Education

Send all inquiries to:
McGraw-Hill Education
8787 Orion Place
Columbus, OH 43240

Andy turned around. The chair was not knocking, and drapes were not swaying. The tablecloth was not floating. The hat was not tipping. It was not dark and scary in there. Rainbows danced in the room.

Andy felt a breeze. He found a broken window. He put in the new window. It fit perfectly.

Andy Lee the Timid

Andy Lee was a timid man. He was also an artist and made stained glass windows. His glass made rainbows dance in rooms.

One day, Andy made a window pane for an inn. He took the window pane to an inn that was far away. Timid Andy walked and walked.

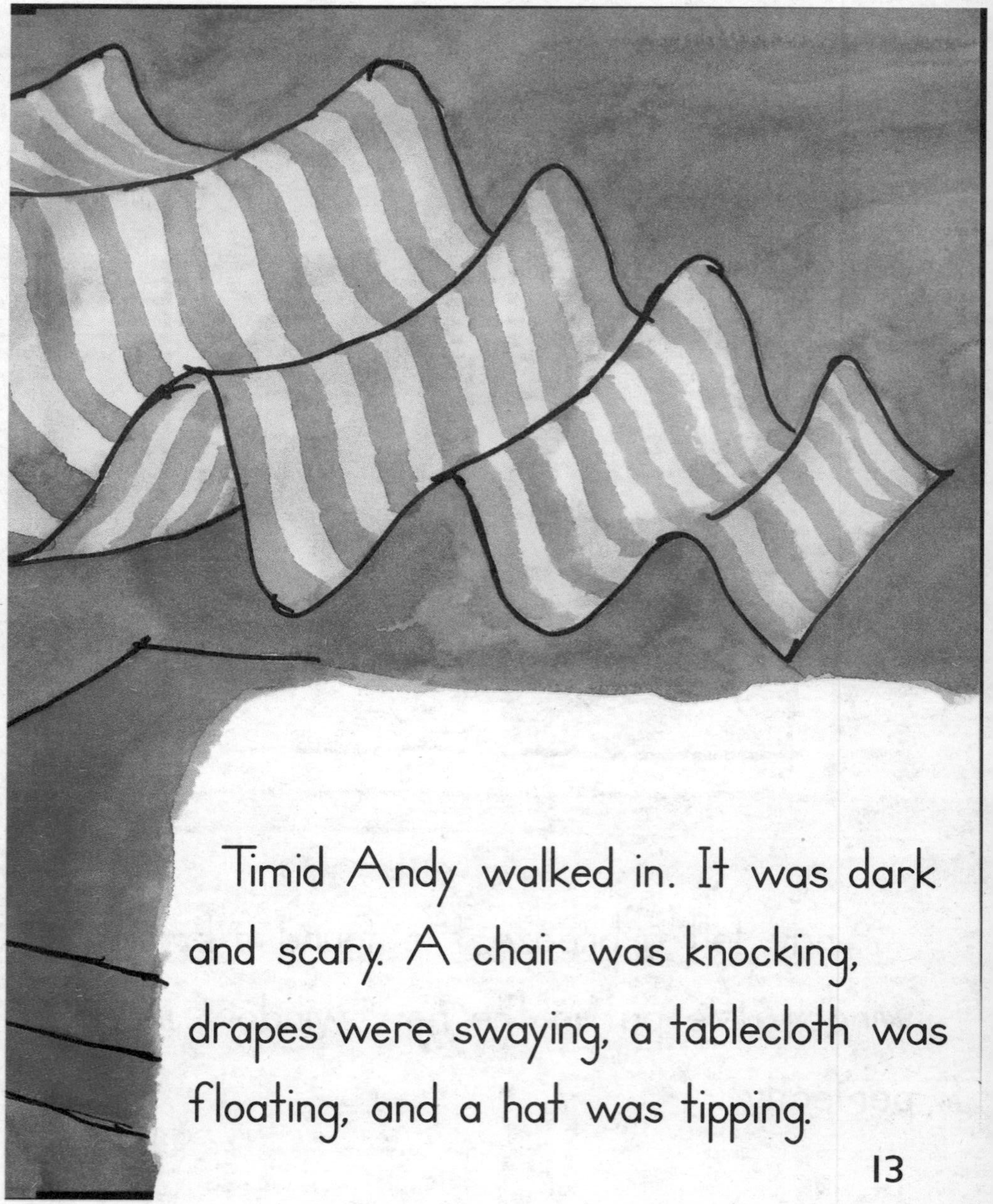

Timid Andy walked in. It was dark and scary. A chair was knocking, drapes were swaying, a tablecloth was floating, and a hat was tipping.

Andy came to the town where the inn was. Down the street ran a maid.

"Turn back!" she cried. "Do not go! A chair is knocking. Drapes are swaying. It's dark and awful in that inn!"

"Stay with me," whispered timid Andy.

Andy Lee the Brave

Andy, the maid, and the cook stood at the entrance. Out ran an innkeeper.

"Turn back!" she cried. "A chair is knocking. Drapes are swaying. A tablecloth is floating, and a hat is tipping. It's dark and scary in here!"

"But what about the window?" asked Andy. "I am a timid man, but this is my best window ever. I will still put in my window."

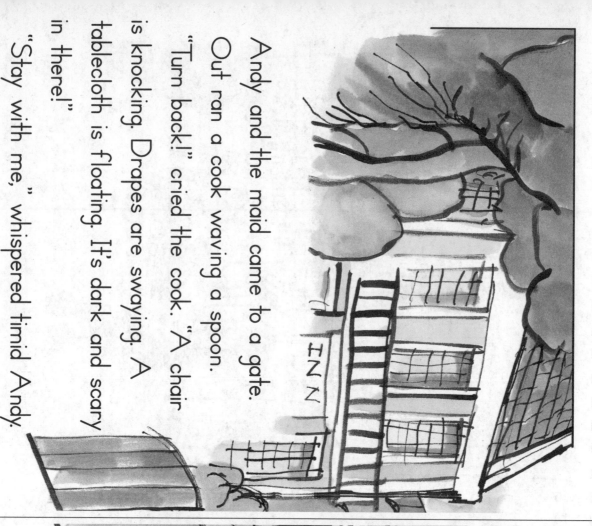

Andy and the maid came to a gate. Out ran a cook waving a spoon.

"Turn back!" cried the cook. "A chair is knocking. Drapes are swaying. A tablecloth is floating. It's dark and scary in there!"

"Stay with me," whispered timid Andy.